Foundations for Growing Christians

Basics for new Christians and reminders for the rest

by Doy Moyer

Contents

Introduction 5

1. Meet the Bible 7

2. Follow God's Plan in History 17

3. Grow in Christ 25

4. Cherish Salvation by Grace 33

5. Hope in the Power of Christ's Resurrection 41

6. Prepare to Worship God 51

7. Partake of the Lord's Supper 61

8. Know the Church (part 1) 71

9. Know the Church (part 2) 81

10. Learn to Love 91

11. Anticipate the Coming of Jesus 101

12. Appreciate the Holy Spirit 111

13. Let your Light Shine 119

Basic Glossary...127

Basic Bible Timeline 136

Synopses of Bible Books 137

For my brothers and sisters in Christ of the Lord's church at Vestavia Hills, Alabama

"I thank my God in all my remembrance of you."
Philippians 1:3

"But grow in the grace and knowledge of our Lord and Savior Jesus Christ. To him be the glory both now and to the day of eternity. Amen." (2 Peter 3:18)

Introduction to Foundations for Growing Christians

New Christians always face the challenge of trying to process and understand an overwhelming amount of material from the Bible. Trying to put it all together and grow to spiritual maturity takes time and patience, but it can seem daunting at first. More mature Christians face the challenge of keeping themselves grounded in the foundational principles that allowed them to grow in the first place. There is a place for reminders, for going back to the foundations, and making sure that what we are currently building on is secure.

The material presented here is a conglomerate of previously written articles that have been revamped and coupled with newly written articles. The effort is intended to present basic material, but that does not mean it will always be easy, depending upon one's starting level. There is probably far more material in one lesson than can be properly presented in one class period, but that is on purpose. Also purposeful is some repetition and connections between lessons. Ideally, a student will read the material, making sure to look up the Scriptures, then come to class with questions and appropriate observations. The teacher will need to cull through the material and emphasize the most important points, adding his own along the way, and adjusting to the needs of the students in the particular class. None of this is meant to be read verbatim in class. The questions are minimal (about six per lesson interspersed), but they are simply meant to keep our minds on what we just read.

Foundational to this study of foundations is that the Bible is the word of God and that the student already accepts this as true. If not, then another type of study would be in order (evidences, apologetics). There needs to be an abiding commitment to Scripture as the revelation of God's mind (1 Corinthians 2:10-13). Inspired Scripture is profitable for doctrine, reproof, correction, and instruction in righteousness (2 Timothy 3:16-17). We desire to imbibe this word deeply, knowing that our very souls are at stake: "Therefore put away all filthiness and rampant wickedness and receive with meekness the implanted word, which is able to save your souls" (James 1:21).

Also foundational to this study is the acceptance of Jesus Christ as Lord (Romans 10:9-10). Perhaps one might look at the chapters and think, "Shouldn't there be a lesson on Jesus?" All the lessons are ultimately about Jesus. Since He is the cornerstone of the foundation on which we stand (1 Peter 2:6), then He is the vital thread that runs through the whole series.

Yet this is not just about Bible knowledge. It is about acting in faith and trust. James continues, "But be doers of the word, and not hearers only, deceiving yourselves" (James 1:22). We are trying to understand the doctrines that help us grow with an attitude of action. "Go and do likewise," said Jesus to the lawyer (Luke 10:37).

I can think of no better words than what Paul said to the Ephesian shepherds as we begin our study of foundations for growing Christians:

"And now I commend you to God and to the word of his grace, which is able to build you up and to give you the inheritance among all those who are sanctified" (Acts 20:32).

Doy Moyer
March, 2019

1. Meet the Bible

If you have become a Christian, then you are already familiar with the Bible, at least to some degree. For instance, you will already know and believe that Jesus died for your sins and that He was raised from the dead. You have already confessed Him as Lord and plan to continue to do so (Romans 10:9-10). How much one knows about the Bible is one area in which there will be a wide variety of familiarity. Some will already know the Bible fairly well, while others may only know some very basic ideas. That's okay. We all must start somewhere. Since we are wanting to understand foundations, let's start by making sure that we are well familiar with the Bible as a whole. The next lesson will focus on the Bible story. This lesson is about the Bible itself, so we will start at the most basic level.

The Bible, often called Scripture (think inspired writings) is a collection of books written by over 40 human authors over a period of about 1,500-1,600 years. However, due to the nature of the books, we believe that they are ultimately inspired by God. God was able to work through human authors in order to convey His message so that people can know and respond to the salvation that He offers by His grace. As Peter put it, men spoke as they were moved by the Holy Spirit (2 Peter 1:19-20). This is why the Bible carries so much weight. Paul put it this way:

"All Scripture is breathed out by God and profitable for teaching, for reproof, for correction, and for training in righteousness, that the man of God may be complete, equipped for every good work." (2 Timothy 3:16-17)

We should understand that it is not the Bible itself that we worship, but rather the God who inspired the Bible. Scripture is the word of God, and because it is His word, we want to treat it with the respect that it deserves. Why? "For the word of God is living and active, sharper than any two-edged sword, piercing to the division of soul and of spirit, of joints and of marrow, and discerning the thoughts and intentions of the heart. And no creature is hidden from his sight, but all are naked and exposed to the eyes of him to whom we must give account" (Hebrews 4:12-13).

Notice that God's word is very much tied to God Himself. The word of God is powerful because God is powerful. The word of God is alive because God is alive. The word of God can cut to the deepest recesses of our hearts because nothing is hidden from God. This is the force of the Bible.

With that in mind, let's step back and take a basic look at Bible basics.

Two Primary Divisions

The Bible consists of sixty-six books overall. While some Bible versions contain additional books known as the apocrypha (additional writings not typically considered inspired), most of the well accepted versions have sixty-six. These sixty-six books are then divided into two primary sections: the Old Testament and the New Testament.

The Old Testament (some prefer "Hebrew Scriptures") start with the book of Genesis and go through Malachi. There are thirty-nine books in all. If you open up your Bible to the very front, you will likely find a table of contents that will list all of the books. These books of the Old Testament were written mostly in Hebrew, with a few sections written in Aramaic.

There were some ancient Greek versions as well. The most common of these is known as the Septuagint (abbreviated LXX because it stands for seventy, the number who allegedly translated it out of Hebrew). The Septuagint is important because many of the quotes from the Old Testament that are found in the New Testament come from this translation. The New Testament covers from the book of Matthew through Revelation. There are twenty-seven of these books.

The reason these are often referred to as "Testaments" is because they each represent a covenant or expressed "will" of God (for example, think "last will and testament"). That is a bit oversimplified, but the idea is that God gave His will to the people of Israel in the Old Testament (sometimes even referred to as the Old Law or the Law of Moses), and He brought that to completion and brought a new will to His people through Jesus Christ. There are several details and nuances to this, but this is the basic idea.

The reason for the division is based on Jesus Christ. He came, not to abolish the Law of Moses, but to fulfill what the Law was meant to do (Matthew 5:17). The intention of that Law all along was to bring the people to Jesus (Galatians 3:23-29). The point was not to bring another law that competed with Moses' Law, but rather to bring Moses' Law to completion by carrying out what God wanted it to accomplish. "For the law was given through Moses; grace and truth came through Jesus Christ" (John 1:17).

1. How familiar are you with the Bible as a whole?

2. Why is it important to understand the primary divisions of Scripture?

Old Testament Books

The Old Testament books are often divided into five categories in English: Law, History, Poetry, Major Prophets, and Minor Prophets. The books of the Law are considered to be the first five books: Genesis, Exodus, Leviticus, Numbers, and Deuteronomy. These books are also often referred to as the Pentateuch (literally, five scrolls). These contain the very beginnings of Creation and go through the time of Moses when he brought the children of Israel to the land God promised them and rehearsed again the Law for that generation.

The books of history are primarily historical narratives that pick up where Deuteronomy leaves off. They tell of Joshua entering the land with the people taking possession of it. They speak of the period of judges, deliverers who, with God's help, were able to help them overcome oppressing enemies. They also speak of the period of the kings, a period marked by division in which was recognized the northern kingdom of Israel and the southern kingdom of Judah. Here we learn about a man named David, the second of the kings. God promised David that he would have a descendent to sit on his throne (2 Samuel 7:12-13), and the New Testament affirms that this descendent is none other than Jesus Christ (Acts 2:30-32). In the typical English Bible, these books cover from Joshua through Esther.

The books of poetry are obvious for their poetic nature. For example, Psalms is usually a book with which most are at least somewhat familiar. The psalms express praise to God, but they also express one's deepest fears and heartaches. They are genuine expressions of those, like David, who sought to reach out to God and draw closer to Him, even when they didn't understand why certain things were happening. Another of the poetic books, Proverbs, is known for its practical wisdom in contrast to the foolishness that so often leads to trouble. Godly wisdom is key for poetic books, which also include Job, Ecclesiastes, and Song of Solomon.

"Major" and "Minor" prophets are not terms that are meant to say that some prophets were important while others were not. Rather, this generally has to do with the size of the work. Prophets like Isaiah and Jeremiah are considered major because they are large works, while books like Obadiah and Micah are relatively smaller. However, all the prophets were considered to be mouthpieces for God, speaking His word during extremely difficult times. They sought to bring the people back to God because the people had strayed so far from what God had wanted from them. They called out the sins of the people in no uncertain terms, and they were often persecuted for doing so.

These same books are typically divided into just three categories by Jewish scholarship: Law (Torah), Prophets, and Writings. They order the books differently, but the same information is there. This is actually how Jesus referred to the books. For example, after He was raised from the dead, He told His disciples, "These are my words that I spoke to you while I was still with you, that everything written about me in the Law of Moses and the Prophets and the Psalms must be fulfilled." (Luke 24:44). In this case, "Psalms" stands in for the Writings (likely being the first book listed among them).

The Old Testament books provide vital background for what we read in the New Testament. It is where we first learn who God is, where we first learn of the problem of sin, and where we first learn something about God's plan to bring redemption to fallen humanity. Because of what the Old Testament contains, it is very important that we spend time studying it. While we, today, are not under the Law of Moses, the Old Testament background and history lays the groundwork for the New, and without it, we will not understand the New very well at all. Let us never neglect this needed part of Scripture.

1. How well do you know your books of the Old Testament? If you cannot recite the books, open your Bible to the table of contents and begin learning these books. If you do know the books by name, how familiar are you with the content of these books?

2. Why is the study of the Old Testament important to our understanding of the New Testament?

New Testament Books

From the close of the Old Testament books to the opening of the New Testament books, there is about a four hundred year period of time. The events during that time, however, are not insignificant. When the Old Testament closes, the Persians are the major world empire that is affecting the people of Israel. When the New Testament opens, the Persians had long been defeated by the Greeks, and the Greeks had been defeated by the Romans. The world had changed with new powers and influences in place. The Greek influence was very strong, so much so that the New Testament itself was written in the common Greek of the day (often called Koine Greek).

The first four books of the New Testament are referred to as the Gospels (gospel means "good news"). Matthew, Mark, Luke, and John tell us about Jesus Christ, from the time He was born into this world until His death and resurrection. Why are there four Gospels? They all tell the same good news, but they do provide different insights from different perspectives on the various events in the life of Christ. Each has his own purpose, and they speak to different audiences. For example, Matthew seems to have a Jewish audience in mind who would be familiar with the Old Testament already, while Mark appears to be more suitable to a gentile (non-Jewish) audience. They each have different stresses, while at the same time showing us the very same Jesus. He is God. He is human. He suffered temptation. He worked great miracles. While they have their differences (which are not the same as contradictions), they all stress the death and resurrection of Jesus. This is what makes salvation from sin possible.

The book of Acts is really the second book written by Luke. It shows the work of the disciples (followers of Jesus) after Jesus had risen and ascended to heaven. Jesus had chosen twelve men called apostles (which means one sent). Jesus would send these men into the world to carry on His work and message. Acts is a book that shows these men at work. In particular, we read about the work Peter was doing at first. Later, a man named Saul, who had been an enemy of Christians trying to persecute and kill them, was converted to Christ (Acts 9). He is now known to us as the apostle Paul. Most of the second half of Acts is devoted to his work. The book of Acts lays the groundwork for the rest of the New Testament, which is comprised mainly of epistles or letters written to various churches.

The apostle Paul wrote several of the New Testament epistles to churches that he was either directly involved with teaching or with whom he was very familiar. He is responsible for writing Romans, 1 and 2 Corinthians, Galatians, Ephesians, Philippians, Colossians, and 1 and 2 Thessalonians. Yet he also wrote epistles to individuals who had traveled with him. His great care and concern is seen in his letters known as 1 and 2 Timothy, Titus, and Philemon.

The book of Hebrews is anonymous, meaning that we do not know for certain who wrote it since no name was attached to it. Some have attributed it to Paul, while others have guessed that it was someone like Barnabas or Apollos, men whom Paul knew. It is difficult to say. However, the nature of the book and its connections that it makes to the Old Testament are of unquestionably high value, so its inclusion among the inspired books is well established.

James, the Lord's brother, wrote one epistle, and Peter wrote two. John, the attested author of the books of John and Revelation, also wrote three epistles. Finally, Jude, likely another of Jesus' brothers, wrote the short work attributed to him.

All of the books, both Old and New Testaments, tell us a unified story of God, the problem of sin, the need for salvation, and the means by which God brought it all about. The two testaments are interwoven together, connected by themes, ideas, and teachings that all point to the same conclusions: the problem is sin; the solution is Jesus Christ. By grace, God, in His glory and holiness, carried out the plan. It is a beautiful picture of grace, mercy, and God's kindness. Yet we cannot miss the fact that rejection of God's plan results in judgment and condemnation. This is not because God wants anyone to be lost; rather it is because people have rejected God's offer of grace. If sin goes unforgiven, there is no hope for us. However, that's the beauty of this plan: we can have that hope, and if you have already submitted yourself to God's will, then you have this hope.

While there are many themes running throughout the Bible, and while we will often stress the theme of God's plan for salvation, the most overarching theme of all of Scripture is the glory of God. All is done to His glory, including the plan He put into effect to bring salvation. As Ephesians 1:3-14 reminds us several times, all that God put into effect for us is done "to the praise of His glory." By reading and studying all of the Bible, we desire only to glorify God and draw closer to Him.

1. How well do you know the books of the New Testament? Again, if you don't know them well, make every effort to learn them so that you will be able to turn to each book and chapter quickly. Even more, how familiar are you with the contents of each book?

2. Why do you think it is important to understand that all of the Bible connects together? Can you state the overall message in clear terms? How would you say it?

The Value of Connecting Dots

The Bible is a book that is so interconnected that in order for you to gain understanding in one area you must look to other areas. While that may sound confusing the more you study the Bible the more you will see the value of connecting the dots of equivalent text and subjects. The Bible is not a book to be completely understood by taking one passage and formulating one's belief.

John C. Robertson. How to Study the Bible: Robertson's Notes
(Bible Topic Series). Kindle Edition.

2. Follow God's Plan in History

The Bible is comprised of sixty-six books, yet the basic themes and teachings of Scripture unite these books together into a cohesive unit all pointing to the same goal. Each book has its own major ideas, purposes, and audience, yet they come together in a way to tell a single, overarching story about God's glory and God's love and mercy for fallen humankind. This is amazing given that these books were written over a 1500-1600 year period from very different people. We don't believe this is just a coincidence.

Why consider the overall story presented by the Bible? Even though one may hear about Jesus and decide to submit to Him in faith, there is so much to learn beyond immediately responding to the message. We may go through an entire life studying Scripture, but if we apply ourselves we can still keep learning and growing. A good understanding of God's plans and purposes begins by a solid understanding of the overarching story of the Bible. This is one story we can never hear too much, and we need to know it well. Here we will simply sketch out some of the simple facts.

The very first verse of the Bible sets the stage for us: "In the beginning, God created the heavens and the earth" (Genesis 1:1). In verse 3, God said, "Let there be light," and there was light. That light was shining in the darkness, and the idea of light is presented to us throughout Scripture to highlight the glory of God. God dwells in unapproachable light that none can gaze upon, and at the end, God is the light in heaven (Revelation 21:23-24; 22:5). When Jesus came into the world, He called Himself the "light of the world" (John 1:4-5; 8:12). That theme of light begins in Genesis and it is most important for us.

In this creation account, on day six, God created people in His image as male and female (Genesis 1:26:-27). God then placed the man and woman in a special garden to tend and keep it, with only one restriction revealed. In the middle of the garden was a tree from which they were not to eat. This was the tree of the knowledge of good and evil. Why it is called that or why it is there is not explained in the account, but one thing we can know from reading all of Scripture is that God always has good reason for doing what He does. Given the fact that He is all-knowing, all-wise, has all understanding, and is all-powerful, we are hard pressed to second-guess what He does. Whatever all the reasons, we can see that this tested whether or not Adam and Eve would obey God or do what they wanted to do.

The Problem of Sin

When the serpent appears in Genesis 3, he deceives, lies, and tempts. He slandered the severity of God by questioning whether or not God would actually carry out what He said He would do: "You will not surely die." Then the serpent appeals to the pride and desires, particularly of Eve. Eve, being deceived, took the fruit and ate. Then she gave it to Adam who was with her, and he ate. Together, they sinned against God and each other.

The problem of sin has now entered the world, and this results in corruption and death. Genesis 3:5 highlights the nature of what sin really is, and we should pay close attention: "For God knows that when you eat of it your eyes will be opened, and you will be like God, knowing good and evil." Notice what the serpent is trying to sell here. In essence, he is saying, "You don't need God telling you what to do. You can decide for yourself what is right and wrong. You can be your own gods." That's the problem of sin in a nutshell. We seek to take God off of His throne and place ourselves there, telling God that we really don't need Him.

Further, sin is a direct insult to the glory of God and His nature. Sin is a falling short of God's glory (Romans 3:23). Because of this, and because of who God is, God would not have simply said, "That's not a big deal. Don't worry about it." If God's glory and honor means anything, the problem of sin must be dealt with appropriately. That is what the rest of Scripture is about. God is dealing with the problem of sin head on, and in doing so, He places Himself right in the middle of it all. Humankind is not capable of dealing with the sin problem all alone. God is the One who has been insulted and sinned against, and He is the One who must generate the plan to save people from their sins. God will offer forgiveness, but it will come at a cost, and that cost is death. Think, then, about these questions:

1. Why is sin really a big deal?

2. What are the results of sin?

Putting a Plan into Effect

Sin brought curses into this world. God spelled out multiple curses to the serpent, Eve, and Adam. One in particular needs to be highlighted, and this curse to the serpent actually turns out to be the greatest blessing for us: "I will put enmity between you and the woman, and between your offspring and her offspring; he shall bruise your head, and you shall bruise his heel" (Genesis 3:15). While this verse may seem a bit obscure, the rest of Scripture will help make it clear what God had in mind. This is the promise of a special "seed" or offspring coming through the woman who would ultimately defeat the serpent. And who is this serpent? None other than the devil or Satan (Revelation 12:9). The "seed" who would defeat the devil is Jesus (Galatians 3:16; 1 John 3:8).

From this point in Scripture, God has put into effect His plan for bringing about salvation and redemption from sin. Because there are so many themes and ideas introduced in these first few chapters of Genesis, let's just trace the seed promise for a moment to see how God brings this about. This is just known as "the promise," and it is a promise that rests on God's grace (Romans 4:16). We do not deserve what God has done for us, and we are grateful for the grace that He is so willing to give.

By the end of Genesis 11, we are introduced to a man by the name of Abram (later, Abraham) through whom God will carry out His will for all of the humankind. In Genesis 12, God promises Abram that He would make his descendants into a great nation, give them land, and, most importantly, through His seed, would bless all the families of the earth. That blessing promise, we are told in Acts 3:26, is the forgiveness of sins brought about through Jesus Christ. If you have submitted to the Lord for salvation, then you are sharing in this very promise that was given to Abram by God's grace.

Genesis records how God began fulfilling His promises to Abraham. Abraham trusted God and shows us today how we ought to trust God as well. We can share the faith of Abraham (Romans 4:16) and become part of the fulfilled seed promise. But how did God do all of this?

The rest of Genesis shows how God began bringing about the promise. Abraham and Sarah had Isaac, and Isaac later had a son named Jacob. Jacob, whose name was changed to Israel, had twelve sons, and through these sons came the nation known as Israel in Scripture (we are not talking about modern Israel right now). This nation was special to God. He called them to be His special people, and it is through them that He continued to carry out His plan. Ultimately, Jesus Christ would be born through the nation of Israel.

Before the children of Israel grew very numerous, a series of events involving Joseph, one of the sons, brought them down to the region of Egypt. There they began to prosper and grow. Yet, as time went on, Egypt became afraid of the growing nation of Israel, and the Pharaoh turned the people of Israel into slaves for a number of years. Finally, Moses was born, and he would be the one who would lead Israel out of Egypt.

Through trials and plagues brought upon the Egyptians, the children of Israel left Egypt by a very strong show of God's powers (the book of Exodus). After already being spared through the plagues, and while leaving, they came to the Red Sea and were trapped by the Egyptian army until God worked a great wonder. God had Moses hold his staff over the waters, and the waters parted so that the people of Israel could pass through on dry ground.

They came to a place called Mt. Sinai, and it is here where God would establish His covenant with Israel and give them the Law and commandments through Moses. Sadly, due to their continual complaining and disobedience, many of the children of Israel would die in the wilderness over a period of about forty years. The next generation, however, would survive. This is what the book of Numbers shows us.

One of the promises God made to Abraham is that his descendants would possess a particular land, a "Promised Land," and this is what we know today as Palestine or Israel. Then it was called Canaan. After forty years in the wilderness, Moses delivered a last series of speeches, with blessings and warnings, so that the new generation of Israelites entering the Promised Land could be prepared. This is the book of Deuteronomy.

How is all of this part of the plan of God to bring salvation from sin? Notice that the plan of God is happening through an historical timeline. The story of salvation is not just about particular people, but about God interjecting Himself into human history in order to bring about reconciliation with Himself. God is taking a very personal, vested interest in all that is happening.

As time progresses, the children of Israel often show themselves to be very unfaithful to God and His covenant. God is still very patient and longsuffering. He shows much grace and compassion, but He also shows that He is serious about dealing with sin. This means that there are times when God brings judgment upon the people for their sin and refusal to repent. This is seen time and again in books like Joshua and Judges.

While God was supposed to be their king, the Israelites decided that they still wanted a king like other nations had. God did allow this, and they ended up with a line of kings. Sadly, because of sin, the kingdom split into two different kingdoms: Israel in the north and Judah in the south. All of the northern kings turned out to be wicked, and they were finally brought to judgment when, in about 722 B.C., the northern kingdom fell to the Assyrian armies. Judah in the south lasted a while longer and did have a handful of decent kings, but Jerusalem, the capital, would fall in 586 B.C. to the Babylonians while the people were in a period of being held as captives. During all these years with the kings and captivity, God sent several prophets to try to warn and bring the people back to God. For the most part, the people did not listen.

They did return from captivity in about 538 B.C. when the Persians were in control under Cyrus, and many events were occurring in history that would help shape the next several hundred years. Yet all of this was being done that ultimately God could bring about, in a real time and place, the culmination of His plan. When the time was right, Jesus Christ was sent to this earth to die on a cross and be raised up again. As a sacrifice, He could make it possible for us to be right with God again. Through the resurrection, we are given the living hope of eternal life with God. More about this will be said later. Think, then, about these questions:

1. Why are the events of the Old Testament important?

2. What were the events of the Old Testament leading to?

Fulfillment in Jesus Christ

Jesus came into this world with a specific purpose to seek and save those lost in sin. He was born in the flesh as a descendent of the children of Israel. Specifically, He was of the family of Judah and a descendent of King David (Matthew 1:1-17). Yet Jesus was no ordinary man. He was fully human, but He was also the divine Son of God. As God in the flesh, Jesus could show us God in a way that had never been seen before (John 1:1-18). As man, He could suffer and die for us and then become our mediator to God (1 Timothy 2:3-6). This summarizes His purpose in coming. He loved us enough to die for us so that we can be forgiven of our sins. By taking upon Himself the sins of the world, He made it possible for us to be reconciled to God (Romans 5:6-11).

While Jesus walked the earth, He chose twelve specific disciples who came to be known as apostles (a word meaning "sent"). He would send these men into the world to tell the good news (gospel) about salvation. Sadly, one of these men, Judas Iscariot, betrayed Jesus, and this allowed His enemies to see that He was crucified. Even so, God's plans are never thwarted. Through this death on the cross comes the greatest of blessings. Why?

Because Jesus would not stay dead. He was raised up on the third day, and this demonstrates His complete power over both life and death. He conquered death, and this means that we no longer need to fear it if we will trust Him (Hebrews 2:14-15). Now, because of what Jesus did, we can know that we are forgiven of our sins, and we can have the assurance of the living hope by being raised from the dead ourselves and live eternally with God.

This was God's plan all along. Now, if you have submitted yourself to God's grace through faith, then you, too, are sharing in the blessing that was promised all those years ago to Abraham.

"But when the fullness of time had come, God sent forth his Son, born of woman, born under the law, to redeem those who were under the law, so that we might receive adoption as sons. And because you are sons, God has sent the Spirit of his Son into our hearts, crying, 'Abba! Father!' So you are no longer a slave, but a son, and if a son, then an heir through God." (Galatians 4:4-7)

"See what kind of love the Father has given to us, that we should be called children of God; and so we are" (1 John 3:1).

1. Why did Jesus come into this world?

2. What benefit do you receive through trusting Jesus?

3. Grow in Christ

Having been reminded of the basic plan God put into effect for salvation, we now wish to summarize some basic issues for our growth in Christ. But first, let's review what got us to this point.

1. We recognized our sin. The need for salvation results from the fact that all have sinned and fall short of God's glory (Romans 3:23). Sin causes spiritual death and separation from God. Before one can receive God's forgiveness, there must be a recognition of being dead in sins (Ephesians 2:1).

2. We responded in faith. Biblical faith is trust. It is taking God at His word, and faith comes through hearing the word of God (Romans 10:17). Once we hear what God's word says, we must choose to believe and act upon it because through faith, we have access to the grace of God through Jesus Christ (Romans 5:1-2). Among other important matters, we believed that Jesus was raised from the dead (Romans 10:9-10).

3. We repented of our sin. Knowing how bad sin is, we realized the need to turn from it toward God. God commands all people to repent (Acts 17:30-31). He does not want us to continue living a life that is opposed to His will. If we take God at His word, we will want to remove ourselves from a sinful life.

4. We confessed Jesus as Lord. Confession of Jesus as Lord results in salvation because we are declaring that Jesus is our king and we are willing to do whatever He says (Romans 10:9). If we call Him "Lord," then we must do His will (Luke 6:46; Matthew 7:21-23). This confession is not just one time, but a lifetime of showing that Jesus is our Lord.

5. We were baptized into Christ and raised to walk a new life. If we want to complete our response of faith, we will be immersed in water to have our sins washed away (Acts 2:38; Acts 22:16). There is nothing meritorious in this. Yet baptism is commanded by God, and if we are going to take Him at His word, then we are going to do it for the reasons that He states. When we are baptized, we are not relying on ourselves for salvation; we are relying upon the working of God (Colossians 2:11-13). This, in turn, means that we are raised up to walk a new life (Romans 6:3-5). All things have changed and become new. We must never turn our backs on Him. We must not cast away the confidence that we have as His children (Hebrew 10:35).

The life of a Christian is worthwhile. Since Jesus was raised from the dead, we may know that our toil for Him is not in vain (1 Corinthians 15:58). As Christians, we have the hope laid up in heaven, the help of God, the forgiveness of sins, and the fellowship of godly people. God does not want anyone to perish (2 Peter 3:9).

Staying on the right track

Being a Christian means a commitment to a life of growth. The Scriptures teach that we are to desire the pure milk of the word that we might grow unto salvation (1 Peter 2:2). This requires a maturing process whereby we gain wisdom and the ability to discern good and evil (Hebrews 5:14). Without growth, we die. We are making a life-time covenant with God that we will continue to seek Him, learn from Him, and do His will (see Ezra 7:10).

Here, then, are some of the fundamental needs that we all have:

1. Knowledge (2 Peter 1:5-6). Learning is not a one-time action. Once we begin to learn and appreciate the knowledge, we will develop a thirst for more. Knowledge of God's will is generally lacking today, and we need to determine that we will learn more. We must be a people of the book, knowledgeable, and able to go to the Scriptures and point to God's revealed will. Work hard at study so that you can handle the Scriptures accurately (Acts 17:11; 2 Timothy 2:15).

2. Growth. We speak here of growing in all aspects of faith. The apostle Peter spoke of making every effort to add to our faith virtue, knowledge, self-control, steadfastness, godliness, and brotherly love. He then said, "For if these qualities are yours and are increasing, they keep you from being ineffective or unfruitful in the knowledge of our Lord Jesus Christ" (2 Peter 1:5-8).

All of these function together like a beautiful orchestra of character. We do not lay aside one of these traits to put on the next one, but rather while our faith is still growing, we add more virtue, knowledge, and so on. Issues that hinder growth, such as selfishness, worldliness, and lack of commitment must be put away. Let us, then, resolve to grow in the grace and knowledge of the Lord (2 Peter 3:18).

3. Prayer (1 Thessalonians 5:17; Luke 18:1). Prayer is vital to our lives. It is a mark of a spiritual person (Colossians 3:2; 4:2). We need to spend time in prayer praising God (Acts 4:24), giving thanks to Him (1 Thessalonians 5:18), asking of Him (Matthew 7:12), interceding for others (1 Timothy 2:1-4), and confessing our sins (1 John 1:9). Prayer is something we need to make time for, resolving to do it because it won't happen accidentally. We need to set aside time purposefully. If we struggle with how to pray or with what to say, the Psalms provides such powerful examples from which we may learn how to pour out our hearts to God.

4. Efforts to teach others (Matthew 28:19). Evangelism, reaching out to others, is a struggle for every generation. We are in the business of teaching and persuading others (2 Corinthians 5:11).

We need to be doing this by our example (Matthew 5:14-16) and our words (Colossians 4:6). The early church took this seriously (Acts 8:4), and so must we if we are going to see any growth. God wants everyone to hear the gospel and be saved (1 Timothy 2:4). Please, don't leave it up to a few. Make that effort yourself. Is there not one person you can share the gospel with? One person who will study with you? Have you asked? Will you try?

5. Participation (Ephesians 4:16). To have proper growth of His body, each individual must do his or her part. We need those who will teach, encourage, give of time and money, sing, lead, and help in the assemblies. Don't wait for someone else to do it. This is not a show; just do your best. At the same time, this is not just about who can or will serve in a public capacity. Great service takes place "behind the scenes" by those who desire no accolades. God knows what we are doing, but never can we afford to simply sit back and let everyone else do the work. Be willing participants in the work.

1. How important is staying on the right track once you have been saved?

2. What can you do to make sure that you are growing properly?

Incentives for serving God

Knowing God's plan, responding in faith, and dedicated to growth, let's remind ourselves of some incentives to stay on course.

What is the Christian's incentive in serving God? Is it the reward of being with God eternally? Is it the avoidance of hell? Is it Both? Is there more? There is no denying that both reward and punishment serve as motivators. Yet, while we would never deny that we ought to want to be with God, and we should want to avoid hell at all costs, there is more to consider. Here are three more ways to think about proper incentives in serving God:

An incentive founded upon love. "We love because He first loved us" (1 John 4:19). When we recognize His love for us and how much He has done for us out of His grace and love, we should respond with love. The incentive here is that of humble submission in response to God's grace. The "greatest commandment" is to love God with all the heart, soul, strength, and mind (Mark 12:29-30). We choose to obey Him as a recognition of His grace toward us. Jesus stated, "If you love Me, you will keep My commandments" (John 14:15).

An incentive founded upon proper respect. We are told to "fear the Lord." The fear of the Lord is the beginning of knowledge and wisdom (Prov 1:7; 9:10), and is called "the whole of man" (Ecc 12:13-14). While fear (in the trembling sense) is involved in wanting to avoid hell, the fuller sense of "fear" involves reverence and respect. If we recognize who God really is, as the glorious Creator worthy of all praise, we will know that we must honor and revere Him completely. Doing what is right entails giving proper honor to the One who deserves it the most.

An incentive founded upon gratitude. Gratitude is the quality or attitude of thankfulness, and this stems from appreciating what someone has done for us. Given all that God has done to bring about our salvation, how can we not be thankful to Him? We are to be "...giving thanks always and for everything to God the Father in the name of our Lord Jesus Christ" (Eph 5:20).

Being thankful is not based on wanting a reward, nor is it based on the fear of punishment. It is, instead, based on the appreciation that someone has done something wonderful for us. In this case, God has, through His grace, done for us what we could never do for ourselves. If this does not elicit gratitude from us, what will?

Perhaps this is why those who do not honor God or give thanks become futile in their thinking (Rom 1:21).

1. Examine yourself here. Why do you want to serve God?

2. Why is it important to have proper motives in serving God?

The importance of assembling with other Christians

Sometimes we approach our service to God with questions like, "Do I have to?" This tends to take an approach that leads to the feeling of forced service or drudgery. Instead, we should focus on the positive benefits that we gain when we meet together. To that end, let's remind ourselves what we are doing when we come together as a church. Another reason for this reminder is that it is all too easy for us to get wrapped up in the entanglements of the world, even though they might be matters that are not in themselves sinful. They take time and energy, and sometimes God and His people get pushed to the back seat of busy lives. We've all struggled with this. We don't usually do this purposefully, but gradually over time we allow more and more of the activities of the busy world to take time and energy from us and we lose out on the ability to make the most of opportunities as we face evil days (Ephesians 5:15-17).

"Opportunities" is the operative term. Meeting together is a commitment of time and energy, but these are also great opportunities to learn, grow, and come away with a renewed sense of zeal and purpose. We find the time to do what we value and love, so what is the value of coming together as a congregation dedicated to serving the Lord?

Every time we meet, we gain **opportunities**:

1. To Praise God in Unity with Others. We have been redeemed to the praise and glory of God (see Ephesians 1:3-14). We want to be with other redeemed people so that we can praise and glorify Him together. After making the point that we need to redeem the time because the days are evil, Paul continued, "And do not get drunk with wine, for that is dissipation, but be filled with the Spirit, speaking to one another in psalms and hymns and spiritual songs, singing and making melody with your heart to the Lord; always giving thanks for all things in the name of our Lord Jesus Christ to God, even the Father" (Ephesians 5:18-20). By doing this together, we show unity and encourage each other.

2. To Receive Strong Biblical Teaching. The word of God will be read and taught, whether in classes or general assemblies. In our singing, we are teaching biblical concepts and principles. As God's people, we are committed to present the strongest biblical messages we can. We are committed to Scripture as God's word, and we will hold this standard out for all to hear and follow. As Paul told Timothy, "preach the word; be ready in season and out of season; reprove, rebuke, exhort, with great patience and instruction" (2 Timothy 4:2). You will, therefore, have opportunities to grow in the grace and knowledge of the Lord (2 Peter 3:18).

3. To Have Fellowship with other Christians. There is power and significance in having fellowship *in person* with brothers and sisters in Christ. We are here to share jointly in the spiritual blessings of Christ. When we meet, we will see examples of faith and love. We will see godly people showing us what it means to be faithful. We will see Christians loving one another. We want to develop that family bond, and we need each other present to do so. By this, we will have the opportunity to lift up and encourage others who might be weak or struggling (Hebrews 12:12). We will stimulate one another to love and good works (Hebrews 10:23-25). We need this time of fellowship together.

4. To Recommit ourselves to the Lord. Of course we can do this anytime, but when we come together we are especially reminded of how important it is to be dedicated and committed to the Lord every day. By meeting with the brethren every opportunity we have, we will be showing our commitment and will be reminded of the need to cast off the old person of sin to be transformed by the renewing of our minds (Rom. 12:1-2). We ought to leave every meeting with a renewed commitment to serve our great God daily.

We realize that there are issues that can prevent us from attending (e.g., sickness), and some situations are difficult. Nevertheless, we need to see the value of what we gain when we are present, and what we miss when we are absent. We need to develop a longing and love for the assemblies. Think, also, of the impact this love and commitment will have on our children and future generations. Let's cherish our times together.

In later lessons, we will look more at what it means to know the church.

1. Why did God want His people to be together so much?

2. What can you do to help encourage others and meet with them regularly?

4. Cherish Salvation by Grace

Christians have been saved from their sins by the grace of God (Ephesians 2:1-10). They know that they do not deserve salvation. They know that sin only brings death. Yet sometimes we become concerned about whether or not we can really know if we are saved. We might worry that we aren't doing enough, or that because we still have trouble with sin at times, there seems to be little hope. Here, then, we want to remind ourselves about God's grace and how this can help us in our service.

Can we know we are saved?

Sometimes we may doubt whether or not we are really saved. We feel that we aren't good enough, that we don't do enough, or that somehow we just cannot make it because we are so unworthy of it. Some question whether or not we can have confidence in salvation at all. Hope becomes wishful thinking. Maybe if we are lucky, we'll squeeze through the door just in time and barely make it.

This is not the way God wants us to think of salvation and grace. How assured can we be about salvation? Are we doomed to thinking that we may only barely make it if we are lucky? Let's ask another question. How assured can we be of God's promises?

If we can trust God's promises, then we can know about salvation. Why? Because salvation is a matter of God's promise.

Let's get some perspective on this. In Romans 4, Paul brings in Abraham to demonstrate that the promise of God for righteousness is not based on the Law since Abraham came before the Law. Accordingly, Abraham could be the "father of us all," both Jew and

Gentile, who accept the promise by faith (vv. 16-17). Because of Abraham's faith, he was called the "friend of God." Through faith rather than the works of the Law, he was credited with righteousness by God. God's wisdom in Abraham shows that the blessings of salvation can come upon all who share in the same faith of Abraham.

Notice the nature of Abraham's faith. In hope he believed against hope (v. 18) because he had been told that he would have offspring, though it seemed impossible. "He did not weaken in faith" when considering his condition and Sarah's barrenness. Here, then, is why faith was counted as righteousness for Abraham:

"No unbelief made him waver concerning the promise of God, but he grew strong in his faith as he gave glory to God, fully convinced that God was able to do what he had promised" (vv. 20-21).

Abraham fully trusted what God promised, even though that outcome seemed against all odds. Notice what Paul writes next: "But the words 'it was counted to him' were not written for his sake alone, but for ours also. It will be counted to us who believe in him who raised from the dead Jesus our Lord, who was delivered up for our trespasses and raised for our justification" (vv. 23-25).

Can we fully trust what God says? Can we believe that Jesus was raised from the dead and is Lord? That He was delivered up for our trespasses and raised for our justification? Will we weaken in faith? Can it be said of us, "No unbelief made him waver concerning the promise of God...?" Are we fully convinced that God is able to do what He promises? If we share in Abraham's faith, then we will be assured of God's promises, and if we are assured of these promises, then we are assured of our salvation.

The writer of Hebrews also speaks of the certainty of the promises of God (6:13-20). God swore with an oath and showed the "unchangeable character of his purpose." As it is impossible for God to lie, we also then have "strong encouragement to hold fast to the hope set before us" (v. 18). This hope serves as a "sure and steadfast anchor of the soul." When God makes a promise, we can trust it. Do we doubt God's promise which rests on grace (Romans 4:16)?

Now what has God promised? "And this is the promise that he made to us—eternal life" (1 John 2:25). Are we convinced of this? If so, we have His assurance, His promise, His oath. Will we waver in unbelief or stay fully convinced of this? That makes all the difference.

John also writes, "I write these things to you who believe in the name of the Son of God that you may know that you have eternal life" (1 John 5:13).

This knowledge and assurance of salvation is not based upon how great we are. Our assurance is based upon the promise of God, and our purpose is to demonstrate the same type of faith as Abraham. As the Hebrews writer again says, "For you have need of endurance, so that when you have done the will of God you may receive what is promised" (10:36). And, "we are not of those who shrink back and are destroyed, but of those who have faith and preserve their souls" (10:39).

May God help us in our faith so that we will walk in the steps of Abraham (Romans 4:12). When we do, we know the answer to the question. If we can be sure of God's promises, we have our answer. Salvation is not luck; it's grace, and we have God's promise on it.

1. Why is understanding grace so important in serving the Lord?

2. How certain can we be of the promises of God?

How Do We Approach God's Will?

God's will has been made known by the Spirit (1 Corinthians 2:10-13). He moved holy men to speak and write so that we might know His plans and what pleases Him (2 Peter 1:20-21). Inspired Scriptures give us all that is needed to be what God wants us to be (2 Timothy 3:16-17). This is a great blessing! God did not have to make His mind known to us. He could have simply judged and we could have no just complaint against Him. Yet He is the God of grace and love.

How do we approach God's will? We have it before us. Christians know we ought to be following it. We understand that God desires for all to know the truth, to come to repentance, and to be saved (1 Tim 2:4; 2 Pet 3:9). What, then, is our attitude as we open up the Scriptures to try to understand what God has in mind for us?

We can approach the will of God from at least a couple of angles:

1. Rules. In this approach, we think of God giving us rules (laws) and we have to do them. It matters not how burdensome or difficult they may be. Our task is just to do them. This is technically true, but this tends to approach commands by asking, "Do I have to?" If we determined that "we have to," then okay, we'll trudge along and do it because, after all, we don't want to go to hell. Let's make sure we check off the list. If we don't have to, then we are relieved that it's one less thing to take up our time. There is little zeal in such an approach. Now we do understand that God has given us His expectations, but this approach can easily miss the point of our relationship with God.

2. Grace. In this approach, we see God's grace through the expression of His will. By God's grace He has given us what pleases Him, and our response is gladly to seek to do His will and strive to please Him (2 Corinthians 5:9). Because of what God has done for us through Christ, we can approach God's commands with a sense of thankfulness that God allows us to be in fellowship with Him. "Do I have to?" is, then, not the right question. Rather, our attitude is thus: "I am so thankful to be able to do this." This produces a sense of zeal.

Why is this second way preferable? Think about the way Paul put it in two passages that connect grace with the works that we do:

"For by grace you have been saved through faith. And this is not your own doing; it is the gift of God, not a result of works, so that no one may boast. For we are his workmanship, created in Christ Jesus for good works, which God prepared beforehand, that we should walk in them." (Eph 2:8-10)

"For the grace of God has appeared, bringing salvation for all people, training us to renounce ungodliness and worldly passions, and to live self-controlled, upright, and godly lives in the present age, waiting for our blessed hope, the appearing of the glory of our great God and Savior Jesus Christ, who gave himself for us to redeem us from all lawlessness and to purify for himself a people for his own possession who are zealous for good works." (Titus 2:11-14)

God, by His grace, is willing to save us. What is our reaction to that? Do we think something like, "Well, I have to, so here it goes," or, "Thank God for His grace; Lord, I'm ready to act!"?

Isaiah gives us a good example of the type of reaction we ought to be thinking about. When he saw the vision of the glory of God, he was overwhelmed, proclaiming himself to be a man of unclean lips and living among a people of unclean lips (Isa 6). When the seraphim brought a coal from the altar and touched his lips, he was told, "your guilt is taken away, and your sin atoned for" (v. 7). Then the text tells us, "And I heard the voice of the Lord saying, "Whom shall I send, and who will go for us?" Then I said, "Here I am! Send me" (v. 8). Notice Isaiah's response to the knowledge that his sins had been forgiven. "Here I am; send me!" He was ready to go to work for the One who had forgiven him by grace.

Christians have been saved by the blood of Christ. This manifests the love and grace of God. When we reflect on this marvel, what is our response? Will we ask, "Do I really have to do that?" Or will we thank God for His mercy and say, "Here I am; send me"?

As Titus 2 shows, recognizing grace, salvation, hope, glory, redemption, and purification through Christ will produce a zeal for doing what God wants. Perspective is everything.

1. Why is it important to see God's commandments in the context of His grace?

2. How should this perspective of grace affect our zeal?

Not of Works

There have long been debates over the relationship of grace and works. The issue is sometimes put out as a "grace or works" or "grace vs. works." The fact is that we are saved by God's grace, not through meritorious works. At the same time, we cannot minimize the importance of obedience to God. We need to remember that obedience does not equate to meritorious works.

The view that meritorious works are what saves attributes too much to man's ability to fix the problem of sin. However, from the time sin first entered this world, humanity has only shown an inability to fix the problem. The first eleven chapters of Genesis clearly show this. The downward spiral of humanity testifies to the need for God to do something about sin. Meritorious works cannot do the job. If we trust our own works, we will fail terribly.

The view puts too much trust in ourselves. We become the ones who pronounce that our works are good enough to save us. We may even devise our own works of righteousness, then demand others follow what we have come up with. This is self-made religion rather than godliness. We end up trusting our own works and our own pronouncements about what constitutes "good enough." We, however, are in no position to define our own good works. All we can do is follow God's lead on what He wants. Our decision is whether or not we will submit ourselves to God's revealed will.

Salvation comes "by grace through faith" (Ephesians 2:8-10). This brings us back around to salvation by grace through faith. What role do works play? If they are not meritorious, then what are they? The same passage in Ephesians tells us that God creates us as His workmanship "for good works." These are works defined and prepared by God for us to follow. Doing them does not earn anything, but demonstrates a faith and trust in what He has said. When we do the works given by God, we are not relying on ourselves, but upon Him, if for nothing else, simply because He told us to do them. If we approach the works given by God with a proper spirit, then we will never think that we are earning anything, but, rather, will recognize the truth taught by Jesus: "So you too, when you do all the things which are commanded you, say, 'We are unworthy slaves; we have done only that which we ought to have done'" (Luke 17:10).

With this view, a subject like baptism can be better understood. Submitting to God in baptism is not a meritorious work; it earns us nothing, but is instead a demonstration of "faith in the working of God" (Colossians 2:12). Even though it is something to which we submit, baptism is ultimately God's work, not ours. Doing it means that we put our trust in His operation. When we have done it, "we have done only that which we ought to have done." We earned nothing.

This has practical importance. At times one may feel, "I just can't do it"? When we are feeling that way, it is probably because we are seeing our salvation based on laws, in which case our failure is on display. If we maintain this mindset for long, we will continually feel the sting of those failures and then be tempted to quit altogether. We don't see forgiveness or grace. "I've tried and tried, and I fail every time. I just can't do it. I might as well give up." Law wins out. We are enslaved to sin because we cannot escape the failure highlighted by never matching up to the laws. Works become more ritualistic, more of a drudgery, and this is not sustainable in service to God.

The good news is that we can, instead, see our salvation in light of God's grace. In this mindset, forgiveness is highlighted. We will not think that we can continue in sin (Romans 6:1-2), but we will also recognize that we cannot be justified by works because our sin makes that impossible. Instead of being burdened by the continual reminder of our sins, we are encouraged by grace and forgiveness and spurred on to submit to God's will because we are thankful for what He has done. The grace of God teaches us to do God's will, not because we think we are flawless, but because we are grateful for God's salvation. This, in turn, makes us zealous for good works (cf. Eph 2:8-10). The fruit is sanctification and life (Romans 6:22).

1. Why cannot our works ever merit our salvation from sin?

2. How is the mindset focused on grace practical?

5. Hope in the Power of Christ's Resurrection

The Resurrection of Jesus can be read in Matthew 27-28, Mark 15-16, Luke 24, and John 19-21.

The death of Christ on the cross was God's way of dealing with the problem of sin (2 Corinthians 5:21). Without the shedding of blood, there would be no remission of sin (Hebrews 9:22). This shows us at once both the horror of sin and the love of God. Jesus died because He loved us and desired for us to have fellowship with Him, but we cannot have fellowship with God in sin. Because God wanted the fellowship, He provided a means by which sin can be forgiven (Romans 6:23). This is grace.

God's plan does not stop only at Jesus' death. We are born again to a living hope "through the resurrection of Jesus Christ from the dead" (1 Peter 1:3). If there is no resurrection, then there is no hope (1 Corinthians 15:12-19). The resurrection was critical to God's overall plan. He is risen (Luke 24:6; 1 Corinthians 15:20). Herein lies the message of hope.

Jesus was buried according to the Jewish custom. He was wrapped in cloth with spices mixed in. They took him to a new tomb very close to where he was crucified and belonging to Joseph, a rich man of Arimathea (see Isaiah 53:9). A large stone was rolled in front of the opening, and guards were placed at the tomb due to the fears that the Jewish leadership had of the disciples stealing the body.

Early on the third day, some of the women who followed Jesus were on their way to the tomb to apply more spices to the body. They were concerned about how to move the stone from the opening. But when they got there, they were amazed to find the stone rolled away from the door. Two "men" in "dazzling clothing" were there. They asked the women why they were seeking the living among the dead. He has risen (Luke 24:5-9).

Everything was falling into place as Jesus began appearing to His disciples. The apostle Paul reports that Jesus appeared to many, including His disciples and himself (1 Corinthians 15:5-8). Multiple witnesses could testify to the fact that Jesus, who had died, was seen alive again. That historical reality is the basis for the beginning and growth of His body of Christians. All of this was done publicly, with the full intent to spread that news. This is the foundation for understanding our hope, our own resurrection, and our ability to have confidence in serving the Lord, just as Paul indicated in 1 Corinthians 15:58. The resurrection of Jesus is also the proof that there will be a coming judgment (Acts 17:30-31). By the power of God, Jesus was raised up. By that same power, so will we be raised. This leads us to think more about the hope we have as Christians.

1. Why is the historical resurrection of Jesus so important to faith?

2. If Jesus was not raised, what would be the consequences?

The Christian's Hope is Based on the Resurrection of Jesus.

The Christian is said to have a living hope (1 Peter 1:3-9). The basis of this hope is the resurrection of Jesus Christ. Both Peter and Paul make this point. What is this hope? The Christian's hope is to attain to the resurrection of the dead themselves so that they can live in the presence of God eternally. Christians do share in the power of Christ's resurrection (Ephesians 1:18-23). Paul identified this hope in Philippians 3 and was willing to lay aside all earthly accomplishments for the sake of attaining that goal: "that I may know him and the power of his resurrection, and may share his sufferings, becoming like him in his death, that by any means possible I may attain the resurrection from the dead" (vv. 10-11). He also knew that, at that time, he had not yet attained it.

In Acts 26:6, Paul spoke to a divided council and affirmed that it was for this hope based on the promise of God that he stood on trial. "Hope in the promise" is the key idea here. And remember, when God makes a promise, we can know that He will carry it through. That is why our hope can serve as a strong encouragement, a sure and steadfast anchor of the soul (Hebrews 6:18-19). This is the "one hope" (Ephesians 4:4-6).

If we are going to remain true to God, we need to keep this living hope before us. This, in turn, makes a difference for how we live our lives. Peter reminds us:

"Therefore, preparing your minds for action, and being sober-minded, set your hope fully on the grace that will be brought to you at the revelation of Jesus Christ. As obedient children, do not be conformed to the passions of your former ignorance, but as he who called you is holy, you also be holy in all your conduct, since it is written, "You shall be holy, for I am holy." (1 Peter 1:13-16)

When we were baptized into Christ, we were baptized with a view toward the resurrection. Not only are we raised to walk a new life in the present, but our baptism points to the future as well (Romans 6:3-5). Verse 5 says it: "For if we have been united with him in a death like his, we shall certainly be united with him in a resurrection like his." This illustrates the ongoing significance of our baptism into Christ. It points forward to our living hope in the resurrection (see also Colossians 3:1-4).

For more, consider the later material on anticipating the coming of Jesus.

1. How important is hope in the life of a Christian?

2. Why is our hope tied up in the resurrection of Jesus?

Why do we believe Jesus was raised?

We believe in the resurrection of Jesus and our own future resurrection, but why? In order to help us in our own faith and in talking with others, let us briefly consider the answer to why we should believe that Jesus was raised from the dead (Romans 10:9-10).

The resurrection evidence is founded on eyewitness testimony (Luke 1:1-4; 1 Corinthians 15). There are several independent, first century documents detailing the facts that Christ was a real person who lived in Palestine, was put to death on a Roman cross, was buried in a rich man's tomb that was new, observed, sealed, and guarded, and then was seen alive again on the third day, with the tomb empty and the stone rolled away from the door. Attempted explanations come up woefully short of explaining all the evidence, and we are left with the best explanation: it really did happen!

Notice how Luke puts this in an historical context that can be investigated:

"Inasmuch as many have undertaken to compile a narrative of the things that have been accomplished among us, just as those who from the beginning were eyewitnesses and ministers of the word have delivered them to us, it seemed good to me also, having followed all things closely for some time past, to write an orderly account for you, most excellent Theophilus, that you may have certainty concerning the things you have been taught." (Luke 1:1-4)

"In the first book, O Theophilus, I have dealt with all that Jesus began to do and teach, until the day when he was taken up, after he had given commands through the Holy Spirit to the apostles whom he had chosen. He presented himself alive to them after his suffering by many proofs, appearing to them during forty days and speaking about the kingdom of God" (Acts 1:1-3).

The resurrection makes sense of the beginnings of Christianity. How do you start with a message that is considered foolish by Gentiles, a stumbling block to Jews, and wind up with the beginning of so many believers while in a hostile territory? What makes sense of the beginnings of the church? Consider this further:

The nature of the gospel testifies to the resurrection. The gospel is its own best defense. Read 1 Corinthians 1, and note especially these statements:

"For the word of the cross is folly to those who are perishing, but to us who are being saved it is the power of God" (v. 18).

"For Jews demand signs and Greeks seek wisdom, 23 but we preach Christ crucified, a stumbling block to Jews and folly to Gentiles, but to those who are called, both Jews and Greeks, Christ the power of God and the wisdom of God. For the foolishness of God is wiser than men, and the weakness of God is stronger than men" (vv. 22-25).

Think about the essence of the story of the gospel. An uneducated Jewish peasant from a small, obscure town in Galilee claims to be the Son of God, works miracles, and teaches with authority, thereby silencing His opposition. His enemies, prominent Jewish leaders from Jerusalem, manage to get Him arrested, charged, and crucified as a criminal by Roman authorities. Three days later He is risen. His disciples soon after begin to proclaim the death, burial, and resurrection of Jesus, and from this point the disciples grow and spread to the rest of the world.

A crucified Jewish, uneducated peasant from Galilee is the Savior of the world? Many reject the gospel story precisely because it sounds so foolish to them. Again, think about the above account. Even in the first century the Jews stumbled over it and the Gentiles thought it foolish. Detractors will point to the silliness and unlikelihood of the idea that a man who was crucified on a Roman cross could be the savior of the world. After a good laugh at all those naive fools who believe such a story, unbelievers can then go on their way confident that reason has served them well. Yet it is here that they may fail to think it through.

Let's take another look, and consider this:

There is no question but that the gospel story arose during the early part of the first century. The story is claimed as historical (Luke 1:1-4), with the recognition that if it didn't happen, Christianity as a whole is fallacious (1 Corinthians 15:12-19). Everything hinges on its historical truthfulness. The question is, where did the story come from?

Would the story have arisen from within the Gentile community? Who could think that the pagan Gentiles of the day would concoct a story about a Jewish peasant who would have condemned their religious practices and whom they killed as a criminal? No, the Gentiles of the day wouldn't have come up with it. Further, the charge that the story of Jesus was mirroring pagan stories falls flat when we consider that early non-Christian writers accused Christians of new, mischievous and superstitious beliefs. Why would Romans have a problem with a religion that mirrors their own beliefs? Why would they invent that kind of story? No, that won't work.

Then it must have arisen from within the Jewish community. But which Jewish community would have invented a story about an uneducated, Galilean Jew from an obscure family who turns out to be the Son of God and long-promised Messiah? Which Jewish community was expecting their Messiah to be crucified on a Roman cross? Why would they invent the story of a man who condemned their attitudes and traditions as well? Keep in mind these points, also: a) to claim to be the Son of God was considered blasphemy, so they condemned Him to die for it; b) to be crucified on a Roman cross was to be cursed; c) He was put to death at the insistence of His own people while His handful of disciples scattered for fear; and d) the gospel accounts contain a number of embarrassing facts, including the way the disciples acted, making it unlikely that the later disciples just invented these things to the embarrassment of the apostles and early leaders.

Those who think this is just a legend have a problem here. The story of Jesus would not have come from a typical Jewish community who were expecting their long-awaited Messiah, only to tell a story about His being put to death, cursed, and committing blasphemy. It certainly could not have come from the wealthy, ruling classes who despised what Jesus stood for, and the poor, uneducated Jews would not have been able to write about it so well. Jesus was not a Messiah expected by any Jewish group, so which group would have invented Him this way?

Yet, the story is there, and the irony is that those same details that critics think make the story foolish also make the story that much more unlikely to have been invented by any typical Gentile or Jewish community. Unless it really happened as described, the alternative is to think that a bunch of uneducated fishermen, in conjunction with a very educated Jewish Pharisee, were able to sell a fable that condemned all of them alike, gave them no cultural advantage, and had no other particular benefit (if untrue) except for false hope. Oh, and they had to be willing to stake their own lives on this lie while knowing all along they are lying about it all.

What best accounts for the gospel story? Paul answers in 1 Corinthians 1, in a work written less than 25 years from the events described. The story of Jesus was a stumbling block to the Jews, and it was foolishness to the Greeks. The answer is that the story came about by the power of God, and the historical resurrection is the final piece of evidence that gives it its full strength. All of the details of the gospel are best explained, not by an appeal to any particular Jewish or Gentile community, but by the simple recognition that it is what really happened. Sometimes, the simplest explanations are the best. The gospel is indeed its own apologetic.

"Where is the wise man? Where is the scribe? Where is the debater of this age? Has not God made foolish the wisdom of the world? For since in the wisdom of God the world through its wisdom did not come to know God, God was well- pleased through the foolishness of the message preached to save those who believe" (vv. 20-21).

The gospel is what it is in part because God didn't want anyone boasting that they could have ever come up with such a plan to save mankind from sin. We won't know God from our own wisdom, but only through His wisdom as displayed through the death and resurrection of the Son of God.

Let us finish by reminding ourselves why the resurrection is important to our work. If we can get this fixed in our minds, then we can know that everything we do for the Lord is worthwhile: "Therefore, my beloved brothers, be steadfast, immovable, always abounding in the work of the Lord, knowing that in the Lord your labor is not in vain" (1 Corinthians 15:58). We can have hope. We can have confidence both in what Christ did for us and in what He will do when He comes again.

1. Why can we have confidence that Jesus was raised? To what evidence can we appeal?

2. Why is having confidence that Jesus was raised help us to have confidence in our service?

Hope Dependent on Resurrection

The hope of future life is one of the "things most surely believed." However, the basis of that hope lies in the resurrection of human beings from the dead, for there could be no future life without a resurrection. Our resurrection is dependent upon the resurrection of Jesus. "And if Christ be not risen, then is our preaching vain, and your faith is also vain" (1 Cor 15.14).

Forrest D. Moyer, *Things Most Surely Believed*

6. Prepare to Worship God

Psalm 95:6-7 says, "Come, let us worship and bow down; let us kneel before the Lord our Maker. For He is our God, and we are the people of His pasture and the sheep of His hand."

Worshiping God is one of the great joys of serving our God. As Psalm 29:2 says, "Ascribe to the Lord the glory due to His name; Worship the Lord in holy array."

Worshipping God does not happen accidentally. If we are going to do any of this in a worthy manner, then we must give it some thought, preparing our minds and hearts to come into God's presence in a very special way.

We understand this basic idea. When we are going to meet someone special, we give some thought ahead of time to what we might wear, how we might address the person, or how we might act appropriate to the occasion. We prepare ourselves so that we are ready. Those who participate in the worship activities—leaders, teachers, preachers—know the importance of preparing their minds and getting themselves focused before they begin. There is no substitute for good preparation, and this is true for all worshipers.

All of us are the participants in worship. We are not the audience. We are the ones who come before God and offer up to Him our worship. Given the solemnity of the occasion, we all need to be preparing beforehand so that we will engage in this beautiful activity with proper hearts, focused minds, and in a manner worthy of the occasion.

The Idea of Worship

The basic idea of worship is to do reverence or bow down and pay homage to another. For example, Moses bowed low toward the earth to worship (Exodus 34:8). We see an attitude of reverence, a willingness to bow before God to show respect as to a king. David writes, "Worship the Lord with reverence and rejoice with trembling. Do homage to the Son, that He not become angry, and you perish in the way" (Psalm 2:11-12). Worship is showing proper reverence toward God.

While it is vital that we sacrifice ourselves for the Lord (Romans 12:1-2), and we recognize that all of life is to be lived in reverence to God, the concept of worship in Scripture is used in an even more specific sense as intended actions. Paul speaks of going up to Jerusalem "to worship" (Acts 24:11). Worship is said to have an "object" (Acts 17:23; 2 Thessalonians 2:4), and this is supposed to be God only. Worship can be in ignorance if not directed specifically to the right One (Acts 17:23), and it can be "in vain" if merely on the lips but not in the heart (Matthew 15:8-9).

Any worship of God is to be an extension of who we are (i.e., not out of character for us), but it is still something we do with specific actions, in addition to how we generally live. This is not about worship being confined to a church building. It is about *intended* and *specified* actions as worship, whether individually or as a group.

The Hebrews writer said, "let us continually offer up a sacrifice of praise to God, that is, the fruit of lips that give thanks to His name" (Hebrews 13:15). Singing praise to God is worship as it renders special homage to God, whether done individually or with others (James 5:13; Ephesians 5:19-20; Colossians 3:16). Surely this also may be said about our prayers of praise (e.g., Acts 4:24ff). If we speak of going "to worship," we would generally have in mind these types of actions. When we do what God tells us to do together as a church, then we are engaging in worship, showing reverence toward Him as we do so.

While God is always with us if we are Christians, there is a special sense in which we are meeting with God in worship. For example, Jesus partakes with us in the Lord's Supper (Matthew 26:29); fellowship in the body and blood of Jesus is fellowship with Christ as well as with each other. We all partake of the cup of blessing and the one bread as we share in the body and blood of our Lord (1 Corinthians 10:16-17).

We worship God as our divine object (with whom we share a fellowship), rendering praise to Him in a special way through songs and prayers, through our sharing in His teachings, through our giving, and through our joint participation in the Lord's Supper. Our lives are to be consistent with this as well, given as living sacrifices to Him. Peter writes,

"And coming to Him as to a living stone which has been rejected by men, but is choice and precious in the sight of God, you also, as living stones, are being built up as a spiritual house for a holy priesthood, to offer up spiritual sacrifices acceptable to God through Jesus Christ" (1 Peter 2:4-5).

Our concern is to offer up to God spiritual sacrifices acceptable to Him. God is the One who determines what is acceptable, which is why we must pay attention to His revealed will, His authority, and strive to do it His way. Now, though, we want to focus more on what it takes to prepare the heart to worship God acceptably.

1. What does it mean to worship God?

2. Why is it important to worship beyond living your life as a sacrifice?

We Need a Prepared Heart.

Jesus rebuked the Pharisees in Matthew 15:8, quoting Isaiah 29:13, "This people honors Me with their lips, but their heart is far away from Me." Assuming that we are engaging in the right actions, it is still possible to render our actions meaningless if our hearts are not where they ought to be. This means we need to be very careful about how we approach our worship to God. We need to check our hearts first.

Remember what Paul warned about in 1 Corinthians 11 while taking the Lord's Supper: "Therefore whoever eats the bread or drinks the cup of the Lord in an unworthy manner, shall be guilty of the body and the blood of the Lord. But a man must examine himself, and in so doing he is to eat of the bread and drink of the cup. For he who eats and drinks, eats and drinks judgment to himself if he does not judge the body rightly" (vv. 27-29).

Whatever we do, however we do it, we must get our hearts and minds ready to approach God lest we find ourselves too distracted with other matters.

Preparation Begins at Home.

Here are some suggestions. We realize that people prepare in different ways, but there are still some practical applications that we might do well to think about.

The night before. If we stay out real late the night before, what are we going to be like the next morning? Will we oversleep and miss out? Why not try to get to bed early enough to be well rested so that when you do come to the assembly, your mind can be fresh and ready to worship God?

The morning of. Think of this scenario: We wake up a bit late, jump up and rush to get ready. The family is scurrying about, tripping over each other, trying to eat, and things are a bit chaotic. We throw on our dress clothes, run to the car, and may even be a little perturbed, snapping a bit at each other. We might even have a little argument on the way to the building, trying to find someone to blame for why we didn't get up in time.

We need a way to calmly prepare our minds before entering into worship. Come in early if possible. Give yourself quiet time, rest time, and get your sleep. Train yourself to get up early enough Sunday morning so that you aren't rushed. Give time to read the Scriptures, study a lesson, and pray.

Personal prayer time is critical. Think about the example of Jesus. There were times He went away alone to pray. "After He had sent the crowds away, He went up on the mountain by Himself to pray; and when it was evening, He was there alone" (Matt 14:23).

When He was going to the cross, He went to the garden, a secluded place, in order to pray. He found a way to get alone and focus His mind on what was about to happen. The point is that before we ever assemble, preparation needs to have already been underway. Don't wait until you get here to start thinking about what you're doing here. As Peter said in 1 Peter 1:13, "Prepare your minds for action." While that is about the way we live and face the world, the point is still the same. Our minds need to be prepared to act in worship to God, and this happens through purposeful and planned effort.

Bear in mind that, most likely, you are part of a process that involves others as well. Parents have a responsibility to help their children learn how to prepare to worship God, as part of training them up in the discipline and instruction of the Lord (Ephesians 6:4). Husbands and wives are to help each other. One person's bad attitude in a household can destroy the mood of the entire family and may result in worship that is rendered vain because we haven't coped with it very well.

1. How important is preparation for you as you think about worshiping God?

2. What are specific ways that help you keep your mind focused on worship?

Keep an Attitude Consistent with Worship.

If worship is an extension of who we are, then our attitudes need to be trained in a way that makes our worship a natural transition. If my mind and attitude is ungodly, or if I'm bad-mouthing people, angry, and bitter, then how can I possibly just flip a switch and make myself ready to worship God? We are now not just talking about coming to worship on Sunday, of course, but we can develop a consistent mindset focused on what is right, then we will put ourselves in a position of having the right mind as we do come to worship.

This is where prayer and thanksgiving really becomes important. "Devote yourselves to prayer, keeping alert in it with an attitude of thanksgiving" (Colossians 4:2). Set your mind on things above (Colossians 3:1-2). Think on those things that are excellent and worthy of praise (think about God the most). "Finally, brethren, whatever is true, whatever is honorable, whatever is right, whatever is pure, whatever is lovely, whatever is of good repute, if there is any excellence and if anything worthy of praise, dwell on these things" (Philippians 4:8).

Prayer and meditation on God's word, consistently and thoughtfully, will help us develop an attitude that seeks to glorify

Him, ready to come before Him and worship. Anything that takes us away from thinking on right and pure things, from setting our minds on things above, from being thankful, needs to be avoided. As we come to worship, we need to refocus our thinking and make a deliberate effort to be thinking on what is right, particularly on praising and thanking God.

Here's a suggestion: even physical reminders can be helpful. God gave Israel various commandments — from the clothes they wore to the way they washed — to help them keep in mind how God wanted them to be holy. Perhaps you can think of ways to help you do this, too. For example, perhaps make special notes to remind you of a passage or two. Think of ways that you will be reminded constantly of the need to focus on God and what is right.

When you get to where we assemble, make worship a priority.

There are social benefits to being together. It is very good that we enjoy seeing each other. We love to catch up, get to know each other better, and I would not in any way want to hamper that. At the same time, we need to remember a major reason why we are coming together. Don't lose sight of the fact that our purpose is still to worship God together. Perhaps remembering this can help steer the nature of our discussions as we approach our worship time. It's important that we are aware of our surroundings, quietly prepare, and help each other get ready to begin.

Even if you personally can prepare in other ways, be mindful of the needs of others who do desire a few moments of quiet, meditation, or reflection. Treat others as you want to be treated. Be respectful of the fact that other people are trying to get themselves set to worship God. Give them some space to engage their minds. Perhaps you might read a few verses from your Bible in preparation.

Don't confuse a quiet respect for a depressing service. Our goal is not to be depressing, but to be respectful and thoughtful as we approach God. We are not to be frivolous. But certainly, in our singing, we should be making a joyful shout to the Lord. Remember Psalm 95 — "O come, let us sing for joy to the Lord, let us shout joyfully to the rock of our salvation. Let us come before His presence with thanksgiving, let us shout joyfully to Him with psalms." We might quietly reflect before we sing, but when we sing, let's really sing! Give it your all!

As we prepare our minds, we don't want our worship to be a confusion of loud voices, but a united voice of praise to God. Thus we are to do all things unto edification, decently and orderly (1 Corinthians 14).

Prepare to Participate, not just Watch.

We are the participants in our worship to God, not the audience. A vital purpose of gathering together is to encourage each other, "to stimulate one another to love and good deeds" (Hebrews 10:24). If all we want to do is be takers, not givers, we may well wind up discouraging others by passively sitting by, unwilling to participate in encouraging others to love and action.

Singing is meant both to praise God and to edify one another (Ephesians 5:19). We sing hymns of praise to God, and at the same time we speak to one another. You do not have to be a great singer. Just give it your heart, and the rest will fall into place.

We need all of us to be active participants in the assembly. When we sing, we all sing. When we pray, we all pray. When we teach, we all grow in the grace and knowledge of the Lord. Determine to be part of this. Prepare your heart before each service to engage in what we are doing. As the adage goes, you only get out of something what you put into it. You may be amazed at how much you can gain by being more attentive to what you put into the service. Don't content yourself with being a bystander. Be a part. Engage your heart and mind.

All of this starts with preparation ahead of time. Make the most of this time and opportunity by thoughtful preparation well before the clock strikes on the hour.

1. How can you be mindful of the needs of others as you prepare to worship?

2. What are ways that you can participate in worshiping God?

Worship as Part of the Church

Worship serves the indispensable function of uniting us with "all the saints," living and dead. In fact one of the most important things that worship accomplishes is to remind us that we worship not merely as a congregation or a church, but as part of the church, the people of God. John reminds his readers that their worship is a participation in the unceasing celestial praise of God. So too, the worship of God's people today finds its place "in the middle" of a throng representing every people and nation, tribe and tongue.

D.A. Carson, ed. Worship by the Book. Zondervan, p. 23.

7. Partake of the Lord's Supper

The Lord's Supper is a period of time during our first day of the week assembly in which we take, together, unleavened bread and fruit of the vine (e.g., grape juice). Why do we do this? What is the significance of it? Why is it important for us to engage in this together? After all, it's not like we get filled up with food.

It should not surprise you to know that the Lord's Supper is, primarily, a symbolic activity. It is filled with meaning, and we are taught in Scripture that we need to carefully examine ourselves as we partake of it. Let us, then, try to understand the purpose of the Lord's Supper as it is such an integral part of what we do.

The Lord's Supper and Covenant

"While they were eating, Jesus took some bread, and after a blessing, He broke it and gave it to the disciples, and said, 'Take, eat; this is My body.' And when He had taken a cup and given thanks, He gave it to them, saying, "Drink from it, all of you; for this is My blood of the covenant, which is poured out for many for forgiveness of sins. But I say to you, I will not drink of this fruit of the vine from now on until that day when I drink it new with you in My Father's kingdom." (Matthew 26:26-29; cf. also Luke 22:14-20; Mark 14:22-25).

The Lord's Supper is a memorial activity, and, for Christians, it is the greatest of memorials. In the Lord's Supper, we partake of the

---

Note: most of the first section on the Lord's Supper and Covenant also appears in *Beneath the Cross: Essays and Reflections on the Lord's Supper*, ed. By Jady Copeland and Nathan Ward (DeWard Publishing Co., 2008).

body and blood of the Lord, knowing that He died for our sins and offers us forgiveness. What a great blessing it is to know that we are communing with the Lord and His people (1 Corinthians 10:16-17)!

One of the marvelous features of the the Lord's Supper is that it is rooted in the Passover event in the Old Testament. What is the Passover? You can read about this in Exodus 12-13. When God sent Moses to bring the children of Israel out of Egypt, Pharaoh, king of Egypt resisted. Plagues were sent upon Egypt as a result, but the very last plague was the one that finally made the difference. This entailed the death of the firstborn of every family and beast. However, God gave Israel a way to be saved from death. They were to follow specific instructions about taking blood of a lamb and putting it on their doorposts. When death came through the land, God would "pass over" the houses that had the blood of the lamb on it. The concept of the "blood of the lamb," then, becomes significant for salvation. The Passover became an annual memorial feast for the people of Israel to celebrate that salvation and for coming out of slavery. This was done in connection with the feast of unleavened bread.

Jesus gave instructions for the Lord's Supper specifically in conjunction with the Passover meal (Matthew 26:17-29). This highlights the typological significance of the Passover and its subsequent events of the Exodus all the way to Sinai and the giving of the covenant. Christ our Passover, the perfect Lamb of God, takes away the sins of the world as He initiated an even greater covenant of forgiveness (1 Corinthians 5:7; John 1:29). This new covenant is in His blood (Luke 22:19), and the shedding of His blood means forgiveness for us.

"For it was fitting for us to have such a high priest, holy, innocent, undefiled, separated from sinners and exalted above the heavens; who does not need daily, like those high priests, to offer up sacrifices, first for His own sins and then for the sins of the people, because this He did once for all when He offered up Himself" (Hebrews 7:26-27).

The Lord's Supper is tied to a covenant way of life. Basically, a covenant is a treaty or contract; the term is used of a legally binding obligation. It is an agreement into which two or more parties enter, and this idea runs throughout Scripture. God makes covenants and He expects His people to keep them. God will certainly keep His promises of the covenant He makes.

To the Israelites, the Passover and Exodus events meant freedom from bondage on the one hand, and entrance into a new covenant way of life with God on the other. The Lord's Supper symbolizes the same ideas for a child of God today. Christians have been set free from the bondage of sin and brought into a new life with Christ (Romans 8:1-2). "Therefore if anyone is in Christ, he is a new creature; the old things passed away; behold, new things have come" (2 Corinthians 5:17). For Christians, the meaning is even greater, for we are not brought out of physical slavery. We are set free from sin and are preparing to cross over into our heavenly inheritance. How much greater is the freedom we enjoy? How much greater is this inheritance reserved in heaven? "How much more will the blood of Christ, who through the eternal Spirit offered Himself without blemish to God, cleanse your conscience from dead works to serve the living God?" (Hebrews 9:14)

Partaking of the Lord's Supper should bring to our minds our covenant relationship with God. When Moses spoke all the words of the covenant to the people, the people answered, "All the words which the LORD has spoken we will do, and we will be obedient!" Moses then took the blood of the sacrifice and sprinkled it on the people (Exodus 24:1-8). Now we have been sprinkled with the blood of the Son of God. Our reaction should be the same: we will be obedient! We have been cleansed to serve. So while we reflect on what Christ did for us on the cross, let us also reflect on our part of the covenant. Does the cross motivate us to work harder for Him? How much will I serve in the coming week? How grateful will I be for the shedding of Jesus' blood? Will my actions reflect that gratefulness? In other words, will I keep my part of the covenant with God? If the cross means anything to us, we cannot take lightly our responsibility to serve God every day.

When the first covenant with Israel was established, the people had to stand at a distance from the mountain. We need not stand at a distance. Now, in Christ, we draw near through His blood, and He draws near to us. We must not shrink back in terror, but rather "let us draw near with a sincere heart in full assurance of faith..." (Hebrews 10:22).

1. Why was the Passover event so important to Israel? Why is it appropriate as the background for the Lord's Supper?

2. How should we view our covenant with God now? How should the Lord's Supper serve to remind us of this?

Why Unleavened Bread?

Why do we use unleavened bread when we partake of the Lord's Supper? At the first level of understanding, we recognize that Jesus used unleavened bread when giving instructions for the Lord's Supper (Matthew 26:26). We know this because it was on the occasion of the Passover that Jesus gave these instructions. Since the Passover allowed no leaven in the bread, and since Jesus never broke a commandment, we can be sure that there would have been no leaven at that meal. The bread at His disposal was unleavened, so unleavened bread was the standard for the Lord's Supper instructions.

Since we desire to follow the example of Jesus and His instructions, then we continue to use unleavened bread. Is there more? Are there other points of convergence that can help us appreciate the reason we are still using unleavened bread for the Lord's Supper? To see this, we need to understand the symbolic use of leavened or unleavened bread.

Was God just being arbitrary about unleavened bread when He gave instructions for the Passover? Of course not. He wanted that to mean something for the people.

The use of unleavened bread connects to both the Passover and the Exodus, events, again, that signified their freedom from slavery and entrance into a new life. The bread was to be unleavened because they were going to be leaving the land quickly and there would not be time to wait for leaven to work. That became symbolic for their exodus and new relationship with God.

Jesus' death as our Passover lamb is also packed with meaning (1 Corinthians 5:7). Unleavened bread was the bread of the memorial of their salvation. We note, also, how leaven is often seen symbolically to indicate corruption or bad influence. That's not always the case, but often it was used that way (for example, see Matthew 16:6, where Jesus said, "Watch and beware of the leaven of the Pharisees and Sadducees.").

Paul uses *leaven* and *unleavened* conceptually, also. While addressing the Corinthian's immorality problem in 1 Corinthians 5, Paul stressed the need to act appropriately by turning such a one over to Satan, hoping that his soul may yet be saved. They were boasting about having this man among them instead of marking and trying to correct him. Paul writes:

"Your boasting is not good. Do you not know that a little leaven leavens the whole lump? Cleanse out the old leaven that you may be a new lump, as you really are unleavened. For Christ, our Passover lamb, has been sacrificed. Let us therefore celebrate the festival, not with the old leaven, the leaven of malice and evil, but with the unleavened bread of sincerity and truth." (1 Corinthians 5:6-8).

This is about the death of Jesus, and the Lord's Supper memorializes that death. Leaven here represents a bad influence that would come from the man who was unrepentant. Here Jesus is called our Passover. John called Jesus the Lamb of God who takes away the sins of the world (John 1:29). Paul highlights this and tells them to "celebrate the festival" (the feast, the Passover, Jesus), not with the leaven of malice and evil, but with the unleavened bread of sincerity and truth.

To see a connection to the Lord's Supper here is no stretch. Just a few chapters later, Paul writes about the Lord's Supper. He quotes the words of Jesus, then says, "For as often as you eat this bread and drink the cup, you proclaim the Lord's death until he comes" (1 Corinthians 11:26). The Lord's Supper is a proclamation of Christ's death—that same death in which He was our Passover Lamb, which, again, highlights a feast we are to partake of with the unleavened bread of sincerity and truth. Paul then writes,

"Whoever, therefore, eats the bread or drinks the cup of the Lord in an unworthy manner will be guilty concerning the body and blood of the Lord" (v. 27).

Would it not be an "unworthy manner" if we are not partaking of "the unleavened bread of sincerity and truth"? Paul is using "unleavened bread" symbolically in 1 Corinthians 5, and that is the point! We need to see the symbolism here, not just the physical bread. Yet that physical bread represents the body of the Passover Lamb. It represents sincerity and truth, and our use of that same symbol should cause us to think of the depth of that symbol. How appropriate that unleavened bread still represents the sincerity and truth of our partaking of our Passover Lamb in the Lord's Supper!

The Lord's Supper is a memorial meal representing the purity of Christ and His shed blood. It represents the Passover Lamb's body offered in sincerity and truth, and partaken of in sincerity and truth. It's not just about what kind of bread to eat, but about what that bread represents. The body of our Lord in all its purity was given as a sacrifice to set us free from sin and bring us into a new life.

1. Why was Jesus using unleavened bread when He gave instructions for the Lord's Supper?

2. What does the concept of "unleavened" symbolize when we partake of the Supper?

Body, Blood, and Fellowship

Paul refers to the teaching of Jesus about the Supper in this way (1 Corinthians 11:23-26):

"For I received from the Lord what I also delivered to you, that the Lord Jesus on the night when he was betrayed took bread, and when he had given thanks, he broke it, and said, "This is my body which is for you. Do this in remembrance of me." In the same way also he took the cup, after supper, saying, "This cup is the new covenant in my blood. Do this, as often as you drink it, in remembrance of me." For as often as you eat this bread and drink the cup, you proclaim the Lord's death until he comes."

The elements of the Lord's Supper are simple enough. The unleavened bread represents the body of Jesus; the fruit of the vine (called the "cup" here) represents His shed blood. Both are to be taken "in remembrance of me." This is a memorial to Jesus death for our sins, and it is a proclamation of the gospel message. We are to do this regularly until the Lord returns.

This great spiritual feast is also to be seen as fellowship both with Christ and others. Paul put it this way in 1 Corinthians 10:16-17:

"The cup of blessing that we bless, is it not a participation in the blood of Christ? The bread that we break, is it not a participation in the body of Christ? Because there is one bread, we who are many are one body, for we all partake of the one bread."

The word "participation" is the word for fellowship. We have fellowship with the blood of Christ. We have fellowship in the body of Christ. We all partake of one bread (Christ's body) and one cup (Christ's blood). Again, this is a covenant fellowship that we have because it is through the body and blood of Jesus Christ that we have our sins forgiven. Regularly partaking of this Supper serves to keep before us the importance of the sacrifice of Christ, and we honor Him in keeping His will on the matter.

We need to be impressed with how important it is to our lives as Christians to participate in the Lord's Supper with a local group of Christians on the first day of the week. This is what we see Christians doing in the first century (Acts 20:7), and other early Christians testify to this practice as well. When we continue in the practice today, we are simply following what we see that the Lord desired from the beginning of His church.

1. What do the bread and cup signify? Why is this so important to us as Christians?

2. Why is it important to understand that we are having fellowship when we partake of the Lord's Supper? What, and who, is our fellowship with?

"In Remembrance of Me"

Just as the old Passover was first observed in expectation of deliverance from Egyptian slavery, this new feast was instituted in expectation of the deliverance from sin that would be accomplished the following day on the cross. And just as the Old Testament Passover was to be repeated annually as a memorial, so the Lord's Supper was to be repeated as a memorial. "This do," He said, "as often as you drink it, in remembrance of Me" (1 Cor 11.25).

Sewell Hall. He Died for Me: Passover and the Lord. In Beneath the Cross: Essays and Reflections on the Lord's Supper . DeWard Publishing Company.

8. Know the Church (part 1)

Can we simply be Christians?

Religion seems so confusing. Look around and we see hundreds of church buildings with various names. Investigate further and you'll find that these various churches often teach very different doctrines. If you are like many, you might be fed up with everything that is done in the name of religion. People are tired of the confusion. They tire of the division. They tire of churches that are constantly fighting over what positions they should take or how they should vote on moral issues. How does a person know what to do and where to go? Whom shall we believe? It seems hopeless, and it seems fewer are standing on very solid ground.

The divisions that exist in the religious world do not represent what God wants. Jesus prayed, concerning all believers, "that they all may be one, as You, Father, are in Me, and I in You; that they also may be one in Us, that the world may believe that You sent Me" (John 17:21).

Jesus prayed for unity among believers, and the apostles taught the need for unity. Paul urged disciples to be "eager to maintain the unity of the Spirit in the bond of peace." (Ephesians 4:3). We are to teach, serve, and grow "until we all attain to the unity of the faith and of the knowledge of the Son of God" (Ephesians 4:13), which is a mark of spiritual maturity. Paul also wrote, "And above all these put on love, which binds everything together in perfect harmony. And let the peace of Christ rule in your hearts, to which indeed you were called in one body. And be thankful" (Colossians 3:14-15).

When we see the religious world full of divisions and denominationalism among those professing faith in Christ, then we know it is not what Jesus wants, nor is it what the apostles taught. We recognize that the unity disciples seek ought to be founded upon the teachings of Christ's word, not upon our own desires. We also recognize that there will be various independent local churches, which the New Testament well shows. That is different from denominational divisions.

Sadly, the consequences of divisions result in the world disbelieving in Jesus. Jesus said that would happen.

Is It Possible To Be Just A Christian Without Being A Member Of A Denomination?

The common thought is that if you are a member of any church, then you must be a member of a denomination. This is not true for the simple reason that denominations were not a part of apostolic teaching. It is possible to be just a Christian without being a member of a denomination if we follow what they taught.

When the events of the New Testament were taking place, there were not a host of denominations. There were Christians in various locations. In their own locations, they would meet with other Christians in order to carry out work that God desired for them to do together. When people became Christians, they did not have to become anything else (which usually requires a hyphen attached to "Christian"). A Christian was just that (Acts 11:26), and there is nothing in the Bible to support the idea of joining a denomination. In fact, God directly spoke against fragmenting off into various groups and identifying with certain creeds or men. Read 1 Corinthians 1:10-13.

Christians at Corinth were beginning to divide and call themselves after men. This was expressly forbidden. Why should we think it any different today, whether it be within a local congregation or in any other setting? God wants Christians, not Paulites, or Peterites, or some other name not even remotely found in Scripture.

Denominationalism is based upon division and is not what God initiated. God designed a simple plan, wherein there would be "one body" (universally) and "one faith" (Ephesians 4:1-6). When we divide ourselves by men and doctrines into differing religious bodies with differing "faiths," we are not honoring God's plan for His people, the church. This is why we oppose denominationalism.

Can I Be Just A Christian?

By striving to follow what we see in the Bible, we can, by God's grace, become exactly what they were: Christians, nothing more or less (Romans 6:3-5, 17-18; 10:13-17; Hebrews 5:9; Galatians 3:26-27, etc.). Locally, we can be a congregation working together in unity, diligently striving to maintain the unity of the Spirit in the bond of peace. Together, we can show the unity desired by the Lord and for which He died.

1. Why are divisions among believers in Christ wrong?

2. How can one be just a Christian, nothing more or less?

A Basic Overview of the Lord's Church

The word "church" is defined and used many ways. Since we are concerned about the biblical understanding, then that is where our concentration will be. Further, when we see the word "church" in our English Bibles, we are really looking at the Greek word *ekklesia*. Since a word is defined by how it is used, then we will be concerned about that usage in the Bible.

Just to be clear, and without going into much detail, we may confidently say that the church is not:

- A Building
- A Denomination
- A Social Club
- A Political Conduit
- A Secular institution for education
- A Daycare Center
- Any other imaginative ideas attached to "church" that we simply cannot find in Scripture.

What the church IS:

The basic idea of the "church" (*ekklesia*) is that of a group or assembly. It is not strictly a religious term. For example, it is used of a mob assembled in Ephesus (Acts 19:32, 39, 41). Applied to God's people, it refers to the Lord's assembly or group of people who belong to Him. We can see how the term is used in the following senses:

Senses of "Church" in Scripture as applied to God's People:

Why does it matter that we distinguish these uses? This matters because it is easy to conflate local with universal concepts, and this results in a poor understanding of what the church is, whether universally or locally.

1. Universally, the church is all of God's people everywhere without reference to time or location. God's people today are in the same body as the apostles and first century Christians. *Evidence of the universal concept of the church can be seen in that:*

- There is one body, and the body is the church over which Christ is head (Ephesians 4:4; 5:23; Colossians 1:18).

- Christ built His church, but He was not talking about just one local congregation (Matthew 16:18).
- There is a "general assembly and church of the firstborn who are enrolled in heaven" (Hebrews 12:23). This cannot be contained to a given locality or time. Rather, it refers to all Christians of any time or place.
- God's great wisdom is made known through the church to the rulers and authorities in the heavenly places (Ephesians 3:8-12). This is not confined to one congregation.

2. The sum or totality of Christians who live in a particular area but not limited only to one local congregation. This is not universal, but is still broad to the region, though limited to that time in that area. It is not an organized group, however, but rather a reference to all of God's people who live in that general region. This is the sense we find in Acts 8:3, where Saul (Paul) began "ravaging the church." We also find this in Acts 9:31: "So the church throughout all Judea and Galilee and Samaria enjoyed peace, being built up; and going on in the fear of the Lord and in the comfort of the Holy Spirit, it continued to increase." This is still somewhat of a general sense, but is descriptive of those who live in a broader area who belong to the Lord.

3. Locally, the church is a group of Christians in a specific local area who have banded together in order to purposefully carry out specific spiritual work. Evidence of local churches can be seen in that:

There is only one body, but many local congregations. Paul addressed "the churches of Galatia" (Gal 1:2; cf. 1 Cor 16:1) and spoke of "the churches of Christ" (Rom 16:16). He showed a deep concern for "all the churches" (2 Cor 11:28). The book of Revelation was written "to the seven churches that are in Asia" (Rev 1:4). Multiple churches show that local congregations come and go throughout time and place.

Local churches are addressed in the epistles. For example, Paul's letters included those to "the church of God which is at Corinth" (1 Cor 1:2) and to "the church of the Thessalonians" (1 Thess 1:1).

Many of the instructions in the epistles are given for individuals, yet there are instructions given to the local congregations. For example, the church at Corinth was chastised for their abuse of the Lord's Supper (1 Corinthians 11:18ff). The Supper was meant to be taken together, yet individuals are responsible for their own attitudes while they do this. Epistles were written to address particular issues within those churches, though many of the instructions and principles transcend the specific epistles. Our Bible study needs to consider the purpose of each so that we can act accordingly, whether as local congregations or as individual Christians.

4. Locally assembled. There is a usage of "church" that indicates a local group actually assembled in one physical place. A local church is still that church when not assembled, but they are to come together face to face also. *Evidence of local assemblies can be seen in that:*

Paul wrote to the church at Corinth, "For, in the first place, when you come together as a church..." (1 Corinthians 11:18). "As a church," or more literally "in church," shows a special time in which they gathered together for a particular purpose (in this case, presumably to eat the Lord's Supper). In 1 Corinthians 14, Paul writes of doing what edifies "the church" (v. 5) in a physical assembly. He wrote of speaking "in the church" what people could understand (v. 19). He references "the whole church" assembling together (v. 23) and provides particular instructions that would govern those assemblies.

The disciples at Troas "gathered together" on the first day of the week to break bread. This was a gathering with a specified purpose (to eat the Lord's Supper).

The letters in Scripture were passed around from church to church (local), and Paul wrote to the Colossians, "When this letter is read among you, have it also read in the church of the Laodiceans" (Colossians 4:16). The epistles were meant to be read "in the church" so that all the disciples in that locality would hear the instructions. This required local assemblies.

1. Can you define what is meant by "church" in the Bible?

2. Why is it important to distinguish between local and universal senses of "church"?

When was the Church established?

One of the reasons it is important for us to distinguish universal from local is that we can confuse the two if not careful, and this makes for a poor view of the church.

Jesus promised He would build His church (Matthew 16:18). Here He was talking universally. Universally, the church was established in the first century on the day of Pentecost (about A.D. 33). While the church at Jerusalem also began at this time, all subsequent local churches are established at a later time. Local churches come and go in time, but the universal body always remains because there is no time and place to which it is confined. The churches at Ephesus or Corinth, for example, were not established on Pentecost, but some time after.

Let us be careful then about how we think, for if we say, "The church was established in A.D. 33; the church was established with elders and deacons," we have shifted from universal to local, and this creates difficulties in our view of the church. Each local church has its own separate time of establishment due to its nature. This does not change the universal body at all, and when a local church ceases to exist, the universal body of Christ remains.

How should we understand the universal body?

The universal church is comprised of individuals, not other churches. Individual Christians make up the body of Christ (see Romans 12:5; 1 Corinthians 12:12-14, 18-20, 27). Note especially 1 Corinthians 12:27: "Now you are Christ's body, and individually members of it."

To see the universal body as comprised of other churches is to view it more like a denominational super-structure. In denominationalism, each denomination is its own universal body with its churches all collectively tied together under some earthly head. When that head makes decisions, these will filter down into the local churches and affect how all of them operate. Aside from living apostles and prophets having authority in the first century (remember, they are part of the foundation, Ephesians 2:20), there is no scriptural justification for setting up an earthly headquarters and expecting local churches to submit. To then suggest that each of these denominations make up the one body of Christ is to further complicate the problem. It is not a biblical idea, but one born out of the rise of denominationalism well after the time of Christ and the apostles. Primitive Christianity knew no such super-structures.

If we understand that the universal body is comprised of individual Christians, we can avoid the denominational structural trap with an earthly headquarters to which all its churches answer. Universally, there is no organization or activation of the universal body. The church functions as each member, each individual, serves the Lord in his or her ability and capacity. Real action can only happen at the local level.

How should we understand the function of local congregations?

Again, a local church is a group of Christians who have purposefully banded together in order to carry out certain work that God desires for His people to do together. The local church is still composed of individual Christians, but these Christians join together in time and place in order to function as a unit. Intention and purpose are key.

Each local congregation was its own organization, intended to have elders and deacons (Philippians 1:1). Elders (shepherds) were to have oversight only over the local group among which they serve (Acts 20:28; 1 Peter 5:1-2). They had no right to go outside of that local group to try to oversee other groups. Each local church is independent of others and is responsible itself before Christ, who is their only Head. Read Revelation 2-3 to get more perspective on this, as Christ was speaking to the various local churches and calling them to account both as a church and as individuals within the churches.

1. When Jesus promised to build His church, what church was He talking about?

2. Of what is the body of Christ comprised: Individuals or congregations? Why this is an important distinction?

Display God's Wisdom

The church displays the wisdom of God, but this also means that we, as God's people, should never try to displace His wisdom with ours. The church exists because of what God has done on our behalf. Let us, then, give Him all the glory and seek to uphold His will in all that we do, whether as individuals or as a unified group of believers.

Doy Moyer

9. Know the Church (Part 2)

What functions did God assign to local congregations?

We are now speaking about the purposeful function of a local church, not what individual Christians may or may not do outside of the context of being intentionally banded together with other local Christians. While Christians individually do many things in their home or with others, it is important to recognize that a local congregation has more specified work given by God.

The only way a local church can truly function is when individual members work and do their share. Consider Ephesians 4:11-16. Paul begins broadly with the universal church in which God appointed apostles, prophets, and evangelists in the first century, then narrows down to the pastors (elders) and teachers who would serve within a congregational level. The real teaching takes place locally as the teachers and learners gather for this purpose.

Our concern is to follow God's will as a congregation, so let's observe in Scripture what disciples were doing in a local church:

1. The local church exists in order to facilitate teaching so that each Christian may learn to serve (Ephesians 4:12). This is the work of edification, building up and encouraging Christians to live appropriately in this world. When a church gathers together physically, all things should be done to build each other up.

2. The local church exists in order to facilitate the spread of the gospel. Paul commended the church at Thessalonica because "the word of the Lord has sounded forth from you" (1 Thessalonians 1:8). Again, individuals carry out the work, but a group banded

together can help make those opportunities more plentiful and affordable. Making a living and traveling to preach takes funds. To that end, a local church may support a man to preach the gospel (Philippians 4:15; 1 Corinthians 9:14; 2 Corinthians 11:8). Paul received funds from churches so that he could preach, and others may do the same. The preacher is not considered a needy saint, but rather a worker worthy of his wages (cf. 1 Timothy 5:18).

3. The local church exists to help provide benevolent care for other saints who are in need. A congregation should first take care of its own members. Then, if the need is greater than another local church can bear due to a disaster or a problem beyond their control, one church may send relief to another church's elders, who then distribute to their members as the need dictates. This is the pattern we see in various passages like 2 Corinthians 8-9, 1 Corinthians 16, Acts 4:32-36, and Acts 11:27-30.

4. The local church exists in order to assemble so that the Christians may worship God together. While worship is never confined to when a congregation assembles, the worship of God together is always important. Christians praised God and prayed together (Acts 4:23-31). They sang praises to God, both together and individually (Ephesians 5:19; Colossians 3:16; Hebrews 13:15). Further, God intended for Christians to gather together in order to eat the Lord's Supper together (Acts 20:7; 1 Corinthians 11:18ff).

The reason that the local church collects funds is because work requires money. We cannot help other saints in need if we do not have a collection of funds to do so. We cannot support those who preach and teach if we have no collection of funds for it. Even providing for facilities that allow us to come together to worship and teach requires funds. That's the reality of doing any work. Christians need to see their giving as freewill offerings that are intended to carry on God's work as He has authorized. This requires that we be careful in the way we disperse the funds. Misusing funds given for specific purposes is not looked upon as good even in a secular organization. How much more so should we take care within a local congregation of that which belongs to the Lord!

Please give careful consideration to how you participate in giving. It should be done cheerfully, not grudgingly (2 Corinthians 9:6-7; compare Deuteronomy 15:10). It should be done as a free-will offering. We make no demands on how much to give; we only ask that you plan carefully as you help the church of which you are part do the work that God desires.

1. What does God want a local congregation to be doing?

2. Why are funds collected from members of a local group?

What is the connection between universal and local?

The connection between universal and local is the individual. When an individual obeys the gospel and becomes a Christian by God's grace, the Lord adds that one to His body of those who are saved (Acts 2:47). A Christian then ought to join with a local group in order to take an active part and have a fellowship within that local context. There are reasons God wants us together, and there is a certain accountability that we have toward one another. If elders are to shepherd the local flock, they need to know who is under their charge. Joining with a local congregation is simply a matter of letting them know that we want to be identified with them and that we want to have fellowship in the work. It's not a complicated process. Even Paul tried to identify himself with the church at Jerusalem (Acts 9:26). Though they were reluctant at first because of Paul's past as a persecutor, Barnabas stepped in to vouch for Paul (Saul) and the situation worked out.

Individual Christians, then, are part of the universal body by virtue of being Christ's people. Each Christian is a member of a local church when that Christian and the group agree to work together.

Does one have to be a member of the Church of Christ?

Think carefully about the nature of this question. We need to make some clarifications.

If asking, "Does one have to be a member of the Church of Christ denomination?" the answer is, "No," because Scripture knows nothing of such a denomination. Or any other for that matter. Avoiding denominationalism is not about avoiding just one particular type of denomination, but rather rejecting all denominationalism even if it uses a biblical name.

If asking, "Does one have to be a member of the church of Christ in the universal sense?" the answer is, "Yes," for the Lord adds the saved to His universal body. The key here lies in how we understand the terminology "church of Christ." We'll get back to this.

If asking, "Does one have to be a member of a local church of Christ," again the answer is, "Yes," provided that we understand how the terminology is being used. So let's unpack that for a moment.

When we use terminology like "church of Christ," we must be careful to be biblical about it. The church is not a denomination. It's not a collection of churches. It's as we have seen — universally all of God's people, and locally a band of Christians carrying out God's work together as a community.

The phrase "church of Christ" is a biblical description. It indicates simply that the group belongs to Christ. Paul referred to "churches of Christ" in Romans 16:16, speaking of multiple local churches. It is not, however, a title, and we misuse it when we attach it as some adjective or title to our language. "Church of Christ preacher, Church of Christ doctrine, Church of Christ Christian, Church of Christ whatever" are misuses of the phrase, and this betrays more of a denominational mindset that needs to be rejected. We must be careful. If we are dedicated to speaking biblically, we must avoid misusing what is otherwise a scriptural term.

Having a particular sign on a building is no guarantee of faithfulness. Our concern needs to be with being biblical and faithful to the Lord and His word. Further, "church of Christ" is not the only biblical description of God's people. Again, think description. We read of the "church of God at Corinth" (1 Cor 1:2), the "church of the Thessalonians" (that is, the church comprised of Thessalonians, 1 Thessalonians 1:1), and so on. There is not just one universal description, so we must be careful not to make this into one when the Bible does not do so.

Understood biblically, one must be part of the Lord's church universally and should be part of a local group of Christians who are striving to follow God's word and work according to what God authorizes. Again, biblical and faithful are key here. Being part of the church of Christ means we are also part of the church of God (descriptive, not denominational), the body of Christ, the church of the firstborn ones who are enrolled in heaven (Hebrews 12:23), and whatever other scriptural descriptions may be applied. It is then our goal to act consistently with the word of God, both individually and as a local congregation.

Here is something to think about. Would a church that is seeking to follow the Lord according to His word really want to put up a sign that is not biblical, that honors a man, or that clearly attaches to something not found in Scripture? Any sign is meant to signify something, so what exactly are we trying to signify? Simply that we belong to the Lord. Make no more out of it than that, and we will be on the right track. We honor God's will by paying attention to how "church" is used in Scripture. Because this refers to God's people, we are not at liberty to change the essential make-up and function of His *ekklesia*.

As those who are members of Christ's body, we need to see the church, not as an entity separate from the people, but as functioning members of that body. When we see ourselves as His body, we will see how important it is that we seek to glorify our Head, Jesus Christ.

"Now to him who is able to do far more abundantly than all that we ask or think, according to the power at work within us, to him be glory in the church and in Christ Jesus throughout all generations, forever and ever. Amen." (Eph 3:20-21, ESV)

1. What is meant by "churches of Christ" if we are talking biblically?

2. Should one be a part of the "church of Christ"? (Remember the above distinctions)

Why is being a part of a local church important?

When visiting with local congregations, this may be a common question to hear: "Are you interested in being a member of this congregation?" Where does this idea come from? Is it biblical, and what is the purpose?

The local church is *not* a country club. We are not trying to keep anyone out or produce some elite group. Rather, it is a matter of knowing who is part of our fellowship and how best to address the needs of all. We want as many as possible to be a part of our family, but this brings responsibilities with it, and we can carry these out more efficiently by knowing whom we are working with. Here are some principles to consider:

1. Recall the distinctions between the senses of the word "church" in Scripture (see the previous lesson). "Church" (*ekklesia*) refers to an assembly, group, or congregation. With reference to God's people, the word is used in the senses of being universal (all of God's people everywhere), a broad area or region (Acts 9:31), local (congregations), and locally assembled together "as a church" (1 Corinthians 11:18; 14:23).

God wants Christians to assemble regularly with other saints (cf. Hebrews 10:25). This requires responsibility. For example, we are to encourage one another (Hebrews 10:24), edify one another (cf. 1 Corinthians 14), and partake of the Lord's Supper together (1 Corinthians 11:18-34). If we do not know who is or is not part of our regular assembly, and who is or is not available to participate, we become hampered in our ability to carry out these "one another" responsibilities.

2. A local church is compared to a flock with shepherds. Paul told the Ephesian elders, "Be on guard for yourselves and for all the flock, among which the Holy Spirit has made you overseers..." (Acts 20:28; 1 Peter 5:2). Jesus, as the Good Shepherd, calls His sheep "by name" (John 10:3). If shepherds do not know who is named among their flock, how can they do their job well?

3. The flock has responsibility to submit to the shepherds. Christians are to submit to elders in a local congregation. The fact that they are called a "flock" with shepherds shows a relationship. The flock needs to listen and submit to shepherds. It is written, "Obey your leaders and submit to them, for they keep watch over your souls as those who will give an account. Let them do this with joy and not with grief, for this would be unprofitable for you" (Hebrews 13:17). How can they do this if they don't know who is and isn't part of their charge?

4. Christians are considered members of one another in the body (Romans 12:4-8; cf. 1 Corinthians 12:14-27). While the "body" passages primarily refer to the universal body of Christ, the various gifts and abilities are still exercised in the context of a local group where there will be Christians with different abilities. We are responsible toward one another, but if we don't know who is or isn't actually a part of the group, how do we function well? How can we recognize and utilize each other's abilities if we don't know what they are?

5. Every part is responsible for doing its share. Read Ephesians 4:11-16. Again, while the universal body of Christ benefits when individuals do their share, there are important responsibilities seen at the local level. How can we benefit one another if we do not know what we can do and what each other's needs are?

6. Paul tried to identify himself with the church at Jerusalem (Acts 9:26). Because of his reputation as a persecutor, Barnabas stepped in to vouch for Paul so that from then on "he was with them" (v. 28). They knew Paul, and Paul wanted to be identified with them. This also shows that a congregation has a right to make sure that whoever is among them is one who will help and not hurt them.

7. Identifying with a local church is simply the process of making it known that you want to be a responsible part of the group. You want to participate and have fellowship in what we do. You want to be with us. "Church membership" is recognition that you are part of our group and will share in the responsibilities. It need not be a big formal process. The elders may speak with you, but this is to make sure we all understand one another and any questions may be addressed.

We would strongly encourage all Christians to identify themselves with a local group so that they and the church may benefit from the "one another" relationships.

1. Why is being part of a local group important for the Christian?

2. What abilities do you think you can bring to a local group that would help other Christians?

The Height of Love

Let him who has love in Christ keep the commandments of Christ. Who can describe the [blessed] bond of the love of God? What man is able to tell the excellence of its beauty, as it ought to be told? The height to which love exalts is unspeakable. Love unites us to God. Love covers a multitude of sins. Love beareth all things, is long-suffering in all things. There is nothing base, nothing arrogant in love. Love admits of no schisms: love gives rise to no seditions: love does all things in harmony. By love have all the elect of God been made perfect; without love nothing is well-pleasing to God. In love has the Lord taken us to Himself. On account of the Love he bore us, Jesus Christ our Lord gave His blood for us by the will of God; His flesh for our flesh, and His soul for our souls.

Clement of Rome (ca. A.D. 30-100), First Epistle of Clement to the Corinthians, chapter XLIX, ca. A.D. 97

10. Learn to Love

"All you need is love," said the popular song of yesteryear. We hear of "love at first sight," say that all is fair in love and war, that love is a many splendored thing, that love will find a way, that love means never having to say you're sorry, that it's better to have loved and lost than to have never loved at all, that love comes when you least expect it, that love is blind, that love conquers all, love sets you free, love hurts, and even love wins. On we can go. How many songs have been written? How much poetry? And… how much misunderstanding?

Here we are as Christians. How shall we understand love? What is the biblical answer?

Love is based on action, not feeling.

Biblical love is not about having a warm, gushy feeling, but rather deciding to act in a deliberate way. Feelings are good in their place, but when they lead rather than follow, they invariably cause problems. Much of what our world thinks about love is grounded more in emotional feelings rather than any real standard.

There are problems with that. What happens when feelings lead us in directions that others don't like? Why won't my feelings allow my version of love? Where will we draw a line? Who gets to define it and why? Either we accept any and all forms of self-defined, feeling-based love, or we recognize there is something else that defines love in a more objective way.

We paved the way for this kind of thinking by focusing on love as a merely romantic idea. We can "fall" in or out of love. We are overcome by emotion and "feel the love." Again, there is a place for feelings, but this is not how Scripture defines or demonstrates love in the primary sense.

The point is that there is actually an objective aspect to love. This is true when we see love as based on action rather than just emotion. Showing love is not a matter of how we feel, but a matter of how we act. Love is tied to action that can be objectively considered good, and *good* is tied to who God is.

To see that love is action-based, read 1 Corinthians 13. Each of these traits of love is based on a decision of the will to act. For example, it is not that love "feels" all things, but that love "believes" all things. The mind is involved and can decide how to act and how to treat others. Listen to the text:

"If I speak in the tongues of men and of angels, but have not love, I am a noisy gong or a clanging cymbal. And if I have prophetic powers, and understand all mysteries and all knowledge, and if I have all faith, so as to remove mountains, but have not love, I am nothing. If I give away all I have, and if I deliver up my body to be burned, but have not love, I gain nothing.

Love is patient and kind; love does not envy or boast; it is not arrogant or rude. It does not insist on its own way; it is not irritable or resentful; it does not rejoice at wrongdoing, but rejoices with the truth. Love bears all things, believes all things, hopes all things, endures all things. Love never ends." (1 Corinthians 13:1-8a).

Paul is not saying, "If I speak... without the right feelings," or ""if I prophesy without the right feelings..." None of these are feeling-based. Being kind, not bragging in arrogance, not acting unbecomingly, not seeking its own, not easily provoked, not taking into account a wrong suffered, rejoicing in truth, bearing, believing, hoping, enduring... These are actions that we choose to do, not simply feelings that we have.

Once again, we aren't saying that feelings are unimportant or out of the picture, but that the feelings need to be based in truth. Our rejoicing needs to be in truth. When truth leads and defines our actions, we are showing love.

Consider also what the apostle wrote in Romans 12:9-18 and think about how love acts:

"Let love be genuine. Abhor what is evil; hold fast to what is good. Love one another with brotherly affection. Outdo one another in showing honor. Do not be slothful in zeal, be fervent in spirit, serve the Lord. Rejoice in hope, be patient in tribulation, be constant in prayer. Contribute to the needs of the saints and seek to show hospitality.

Bless those who persecute you; bless and do not curse them. Rejoice with those who rejoice, weep with those who weep. Live in harmony with one another. Do not be haughty, but associate with the lowly. Never be wise in your own sight. Repay no one evil for evil, but give thought to do what is honorable in the sight of all. If possible, so far as it depends on you, live peaceably with all."

1. Why are feelings not a good guide for understanding true love?

2. How do you see love acting when you read the given Scriptures?

Love is defined by God.

What we are really saying here is that God defines love, not us. On what basis does God do this? The answer is found in God's nature, for God is love (1 John 4:8). Love is not just something God shows, but it is inherent in His nature as who He is. God defines love by His nature, then, and in order to see love in action, we need to see how God has acted.

The greatest display of love from God is found in God sending Jesus in the flesh. Many passages in Scripture make this point. For example:

"For God so loved the world, that he gave his only Son, that whoever believes in him should not perish but have eternal life." (John 3:16).

"Greater love has no one than this, that someone lay down his life for his friends. You are my friends if you do what I command you." (John 15:13-14).

"For while we were still weak, at the right time Christ died for the ungodly. For one will scarcely die for a righteous person—though perhaps for a good person one would dare even to die—but God shows his love for us in that while we were still sinners, Christ died for us." (Romans 5:6-8).

Romans 8 makes the point strongly. God has demonstrated His love in such a way that even the persecutions and distresses of life cannot tell us that God does not love us. Read Romans 8:31-39.

Because God is love, we ought to love Him.

Jesus said that the Greatest Commandment ever given is this: "You shall love the Lord your God with all your heart, and with all your soul, and with all your mind.' This is the great and foremost commandment" (Mathew 22:37-38). This command was first found in Deuteronomy 6:4-6. The context shows that this was to be Israel's response to God based upon what He did for them. God loved them; they should love God.

There is no question but that we should love God. James asked, "Did not God choose the poor of this world to be rich in faith and heirs of the kingdom which He promised to those who love Him?" (James 2:5)

Let's notice, though, that loving God does not mean, "I have this warm mushy feeling about God." This is not about "falling in love with God," as some might portray the idea. The true meaning of loving God is much greater, and this is, again, defined by God.

Jesus plainly put it this way: "If you love me, you will keep my commandments" (John 14:15). If we are not doing what God teaches us to do, then we cannot say that we really love God. The apostle John followed this line of thinking when he wrote, "By this we know that we love the children of God, when we love God and obey his commandments. For this is the love of God, that we keep his commandments. And his commandments are not burdensome" (1 John 5:2-3).

John ties together all of these ideas of loving God, loving the children of God (brothers and sisters in Christ), observing God's commandments, and even, by faith, overcoming the world (v. 4). These go hand in hand, and if we really love God, we'll do all we can to observe these. They are not independent of each other.

1. On what basis can we say that love is defined by God? What does this mean?

2. Knowing what God has done for us, how should we respond to Him?

God's Love is the Basis for Loving One Another.

The way that we learn to love one another better is by paying attention to the way that God has shown His love for us. John wrote, "By this we know love, that he laid down his life for us, and we ought to lay down our lives for the brothers. But if anyone has the world's goods and sees his brother in need, yet closes his heart against him, how does God's love abide in him?" (1 John 3:16-17)

Under the Law of Moses, God was still the standard for love. They were to learn to "love the sojourner" based upon how God had treated them: "For the Lord your God is God of gods and Lord of lords, the great, the mighty, and the awesome God, who is not partial and takes no bribe. He executes justice for the fatherless and the widow, and loves the sojourner, giving him food and clothing. Love the sojourner, therefore, for you were sojourners in the land of Egypt. You shall fear the Lord your God. You shall serve him and hold fast to him, and by his name you shall swear." (Deut. 10:17-20).

Note again how not only is love based upon God as the standard, but is also demonstrable in the way we act.

Consider, further, the second great commandment, according to Jesus: "You shall love your neighbor as yourself" (Matt. 22:39-40).

The context for this is in Leviticus 19. Before giving the command this way, the Lord demonstrates how such love will be carried out. They were to leave some harvest in their fields for the needy and stranger (vv. 9-10). They were not to steal or deal falsely with others (vv. 11-12). They were not to oppress, rob, curse others, or put stumbling blocks in front of the deaf or blind (vv. 13-14). They were to allow no injustice in judgment; they were not to be partial but to deal fairly. They were not to act against the life of a neighbor (vv. 15-16). Then, we read in verses 17-18, "You shall not hate your brother in your heart, but you shall reason frankly with your neighbor, lest you incur sin because of him. You shall not take vengeance or bear a grudge against the sons of your own people, but you shall love your neighbor as yourself: I am the Lord."

Loving neighbor as self is about how we treat others. Think of the "neighbor" in the parable of the good Samaritan (Luke 10:30-37). Asking, "Which of these three do you think proved to be a neighbor to the man who fell into the robbers' hands?" (v. 36) is essentially asking, "Who showed love?" And the response, "The one who showed mercy," shows that love is shown when mercy is shown. Jesus said, "go and do the same," which was another way of saying, "Go love your neighbor." Show mercy. Show compassion. Take care of needs. This is love.

This is what James calls the "royal law": "If you really fulfill the royal law according to the Scripture, 'You shall love your neighbor as yourself,' you are doing well. But if you show partiality, you are committing sin and are convicted by the law as transgressors" (James 2:8-9). Note here how James indicates that showing love and fulfilling the "royal law" is by not showing partiality. That is, showing partiality is an indicator that we are not showing love for others.

This is also tied to the demonstration of faith in James 2:14-26. Faith and love go hand in hand in the way that we treat others. In other words, both faith and love are demonstrated by action. Compare this, again, to what we saw in Deuteronomy 10:18, "He executes justice for the orphan and the widow, and shows His love for the alien by giving him food and clothing." James had already spoken of the orphan and widow, and now speaks of food and clothing. James is speaking of the very same issues that Moses spoke of. Demonstrating love through our actions is a demonstration of faith.

The apostle Paul wrote, "Owe no one anything, except to love each other, for the one who loves another has fulfilled the law. For the commandments, 'You shall not commit adultery, You shall not murder, You shall not steal, You shall not covet,' and any other commandment, are summed up in this word: 'You shall love your neighbor as yourself.' Love does no wrong to a neighbor; therefore love is the fulfilling of the law." (Romans 13:8-10)

Let that last part really sink in. Love does no wrong to a neighbor. Love fulfills the law. Love treats others as we would want to be treated (Matthew 7:12). Again, because God is love, we ought to love God and love one another. Having been made in God's image, God gives us that capacity to show love as He does.

"Beloved, let us love one another, for love is from God, and whoever loves has been born of God and knows God. Anyone who does not love does not know God, because God is love. In this the love of God was made manifest among us, that God sent his only Son into the world, so that we might live through him. In this is love, not that we have loved God but that he loved us and sent his Son to be the propitiation for our sins. Beloved, if God so loved us, we also ought to love one another" (1 John 4:7-11).

The love that God shows us is the kind of love that husbands are to show their wives (Ephesians 5:25-30). It is also the standard for how we are to love even our enemies (Matthew 5:43-48). "You have heard that it was said, 'You shall love your neighbor and hate your enemy.' But I say to you, Love your enemies and pray for those who persecute you, so that you may be sons of your Father who is in heaven. ..." By now we should get the point. Love is based on God. He is the Standard for what it means to love.

1. How can we truly learn how to love?

2. If we really love others, how will we be treating them?

The Resurrection Hope

Can one serve God who thinks that this life is all there is? How can he, for he is unable to look beyond the seen into the unseen, wherein we glimpse the eternal (2 Cor 4:16-18). It is in that eternal glimpse where we find the hope for which Christ has redeemed us. This hope is bound up in resurrection, which itself is based on Christ's resurrection. And just as surely as Christ was raised from the dead, He will return. At that time, all will hear His voice. None will be exempt. Yet if we wish to know the resurrection of life rather than judgment, we will let the resurrection of Jesus change the way we live now for Him.

Doy Moyer

11. Anticipate the Coming of Jesus

"The times of ignorance God overlooked, but now he commands all people everywhere to repent, because he has fixed a day on which he will judge the world in righteousness by a man whom he has appointed; and of this he has given assurance to all by raising him from the dead" (Acts 17:29-31).

The second coming of Jesus is one of the most forceful influences in Scripture for prodding us to do what is right. Yet, there is probably more speculation about this than just about anything else in Scripture.

All we can know about it is what Scripture teaches. Let's consider this lesson to be a basic primer on the second coming, for we will not be able to fully explain or deal with all passages in detail. We want to fill our minds with Scripture and our hearts with faith.

We Believe He is Coming Back.

Why? Because we believe that Jesus is Lord based on His resurrection, and the resurrection is key to our faith in His coming. "But in fact Christ has been raised from the dead, the firstfruits of those who have fallen asleep" (1 Corinthians 15:20). Since Jesus was raised from the dead, so will we all. That is the promise. You might go back and review the earlier lesson on the hope and resurrection.

Note: My father, Forrest D. Moyer, wrote a book called *Things Most Surely Believed*. In this book he had a chapter on the second coming of Jesus. I took the liberty of reusing a fair bit of that outline for the structure of this lesson, while changing a few things. If you get a chance to read that book, it is edifying, particularly for the Christian younger in the faith. — Doy

Jesus promised He would return: "Do not marvel at this, for an hour is coming when all who are in the tombs will hear his voice and come out, those who have done good to the resurrection of life, and those who have done evil to the resurrection of judgment" (John 5:28-29).

The Angel promised His return: They said, "Men of Galilee, why do you stand looking into heaven? This Jesus, who was taken up from you into heaven, will come in the same way as you saw him go into heaven" (Acts 1:11).

Paul promised His return: "For the Lord himself will descend from heaven with a cry of command, with the voice of an archangel, and with the sound of the trumpet of God. And the dead in Christ will rise first" (1 Thessalonians 4:16).

Peter promised His return: "But the day of the Lord will come like a thief, and then the heavens will pass away with a roar, and the heavenly bodies will be burned up and dissolved, and the earth and the works that are done on it will be exposed" (2 Peter 3:10).

James promised His return: "Be patient, therefore, brothers, until the coming of the Lord. See how the farmer waits for the precious fruit of the earth, being patient about it, until it receives the early and the late rains. You also, be patient. Establish your hearts, for the coming of the Lord is at hand" (James 5:7-8).

John promised His return: "Beloved, we are God's children now, and what we will be has not yet appeared; but we know that when he appears we shall be like him, because we shall see him as he is" (1 John 3:2).

What is the Nature of His Coming? What's it going to be like?

His coming will be with great power and glory.

"When the Son of Man comes in his glory, and all the angels with him, then he will sit on his glorious throne. Before him will be gathered all the nations, and he will separate people one from another as a shepherd separates the sheep from the goats. And he will place the sheep on his right, but the goats on the left" (Matthew 25:31-33).

He will come in person — He's not sending a delegate, but will come Himself. This is personal.

"For the Lord *Himself* will descend from heaven..." (1 Thessalonians 4:16). Again, the angel said, "*This Jesus,* who was taken up from you into heaven, will come in the same way as you saw him go into heaven" (Acts 1:11).

Everyone will recognize and know the power of Christ when He comes.

Every eye will see: "Behold, he is coming with the clouds, and every eye will see him, even those who pierced him, and all tribes of the earth will wail on account of him. Even so. Amen" (Revelation 1:7).

Every ear shall hear: "all who are in the tombs will hear his voice" (John 5:28).

Every knee will bow and every tongue will confess: "Therefore God has highly exalted him and bestowed on him the name that is above every name, so that at the name of Jesus every knee should bow, in heaven and on earth and under the earth, and every tongue confess that Jesus Christ is Lord, to the glory of God the Father" (Philippians 2:9-11).

1. Why should we believe that Jesus is coming back? What assurance has God given?

2. How can we know that everyone will know when Jesus returns?

When will Jesus come back?

Many thought Jesus would return immediately.

"Now concerning the times and the seasons, brothers, you have no need to have anything written to you. For you yourselves are fully aware that the day of the Lord will come like a thief in the night" (1 Thessalonians 5:1-2).

"Now concerning the coming of our Lord Jesus Christ and our being gathered together to him, we ask you, brothers, not to be quickly shaken in mind or alarmed, either by a spirit or a spoken word, or a letter seeming to be from us, to the effect that the day of the Lord has come" (2 Thessalonians. 2:1-2).

Many have tried to prophesy about when Jesus will come. They have set dates only to fail time after time. The truth is that we do not know when He is coming. We only know that He is.

Scripture tells us it will come "like a thief" (1 Thessalonians 5:1; 2 Peter 3:10). It is folly to try to put a time on any judgment. Even when the disciples asked Jesus about the timing of His kingdom, "He said to them, 'It is not for you to know times or epochs which the Father has fixed by His own authority'" (Acts 1:7). While that is not about the second coming specifically, the point is the same. We do not know when God will make this happen. Therefore, be ready at all times.

Why Is Jesus Coming?

He will hand the kingdom back over to the Father.

Jesus is not coming back to establish a 1,000-year earthly kingdom as is often taught. Jesus was already raised up to sit on the throne of David in fulfillment of God's promise that David would have a descendent to rule on His throne (2 Samuel 7:12-13). Peter preached this in Acts 2. Paul preached it in Acts 13. Now, those who are Christ's have been translated from the domain of darkness to the kingdom of God's dear Son (Colossians 1:13). Paul tells us in 1 Corinthians 15:23-25 that when Christ returns, He will hand the kingdom back over to the Father, "after destroying every rule and every authority and power" (v. 24). He will not be establishing a kingdom. Rather, He will be returning it to the Father because all will have been completed and fulfilled at that time.

Scripture shows that Jesus could not be a king on earth for one basic reason: He is the Priest who sits on His throne (Psalm 110), as both the kingship and High Priesthood were joined together in Him (Zechariah 6:13). Hebrews shows that Jesus could not be priest on earth based on the Law (Hebrews 8:4). If He can't be a Priest on earth, neither will He be King on earth in the same sense. Jesus' kingdom is very different from one that we would see on earth.

He will raise the dead in a final restoration.

Again, Jesus promised that there would be a day in which all would hear His voice and come forth from the graves. There is a resurrection to come (John 5:28-29).

Then, the apostle Paul points this out: "But this I confess to you, that according to the Way, which they call a sect, I worship the God of our fathers, believing everything laid down by the Law and written in the Prophets, having a hope in God, which these men themselves accept, that there will be a resurrection of both the just and the unjust" (Acts 24:14-15).

Paul specifically affirms that believers will be raised since Jesus was raised as the firstfruits (1 Corinthians 15:20-23).

Further, this will bring in what Scripture calls the "time for restoring all things" (Acts 3:19-21). Since sin corrupted everything, we are promised the "new heavens and new earth in which righteousness dwells" (2 Peter 3:13). In the resurrection, we will then be dwelling with God Himself in His paradise as He brings to completion everything that He planned from the beginning. All will be made right.

He will bring judgment and salvation.

When Jesus comes, He will bring judgment for those who have rejected His offer of grace and salvation for those who have received it. See again John 5:28-29 and Acts 17:30-31. Matthew 25:31-32 describes that scene of all standing before Him and Jesus separating the sheep from the goats. "These will go away into eternal punishment, but the righteous into eternal life" (v. 46).

Peter writes: "But by the same word the heavens and earth that now exist are stored up for fire, being kept until the day of judgment and destruction of the ungodly. But do not overlook this one fact, beloved, that with the Lord one day is as a thousand years, and a thousand years as one day. The Lord is not slow to fulfill his promise as some count slowness, but is patient toward you, not wishing that any should perish, but that all should reach repentance. But the day of the Lord will come like a thief, and then the heavens will pass away with a roar, and the heavenly bodies will be burned up and dissolved, and the earth and the works that are done on it will be exposed." (2 Peter 3:7-10).

Those who perish suffer the penalty for not listening to the Lord and thereby dying in their sins. This is known as hell (Mark 9:47-48). At the same time, those who did listen and obey will find their reward:

"…and to grant relief to you who are afflicted as well as to us, when the Lord Jesus is revealed from heaven with his mighty angels in flaming fire, inflicting vengeance on those who do not know God and on those who do not obey the gospel of our Lord Jesus. They will suffer the punishment of eternal destruction, away from the presence of the Lord and from the glory of his might, when he comes on that day to be glorified in his saints, and to be marveled at among all who have believed, because our testimony to you was believed" (2 Thessalonians 1:7-10).

Those faithful who remain alive at the time Jesus comes will be caught up with the Lord to be with Him always (1 Thessalonians 4:17). If we fear the idea of judgment, then we need to receive God's offer of grace through Christ. Everyone will appear before the judgment seat of Christ to give an account (2 Corinthians 5:10). Will we stand before Him forgiven or unforgiven? God's offer of grace is still available for those living on earth.

1. When will Jesus return? Why do predictions of the timing fail so much?

2. Why is Jesus coming back? How is this a motivation for you?

Because He is Coming, What Do We Do?

We get ready.

Continuing with what Peter wrote: "Since all these things are thus to be dissolved, what sort of people ought you to be in lives of holiness and godliness, waiting for and hastening the coming of the day of God, because of which the heavens will be set on fire and dissolved, and the heavenly bodies will melt as they burn! But according to his promise we are waiting for new heavens and a new earth in which righteousness dwells" (2 Peter 3:11-13).

The emphasis is on being ready. It's not about when. It's not about how much. It's about knowing what sort of people we ought to be as we await His coming.

We Watch.

When we are aware that we will face condemnation or be victorious in salvation, and we do not know when that might happen, then it is only natural that we continue watching. Paul used this principle in his warnings. For example, read 1 Thessalonians 5:3-11. Some will think, "peace and safety," but sudden destruction will come. Yet those who are ready need not "sleep," but rather stay alert and sober. When we are ready, then we can find great encouragement in building up one another.

We take comfort.

In 1 Thessalonians 4:16-18, Paul affirmed that Jesus would descend from heaven and the dead will rise. Those still alive at that time who were faithful to God will also be caught up with the Lord. Paul ends this section by saying, "Therefore comfort one another with these words." It is indeed a matter of great comfort when we know the outcome and we can rest safely with our trust firmly in the Lord.

We stay hopeful.

Paul wrote to Titus, in Titus 2:11-14 and affirmed that God's grace had appeared, "bringing salvation for all people, training us to renounce ungodliness and worldly passions, and to live self-controlled, upright, and godly lives in the present age, waiting for our blessed hope, the appearing of the glory of our great God and Savior Jesus Christ, who gave himself for us to redeem us from all lawlessness and to purify for himself a people for his own possession who are zealous for good works."

Notice that he said that we are waiting for "our blessed hope." God's grace will sustain us as we trust Him, and because of God's grace we will stay zealous to do what God wants from us.

Peter, also, affirmed our great hope: "Blessed be the God and Father of our Lord Jesus Christ! According to his great mercy, he has caused us to be born again to a living hope through the resurrection of Jesus Christ from the dead, to an inheritance that is imperishable, undefiled, and unfading, kept in heaven for you, who by God's power are being guarded through faith for a salvation ready to be revealed in the last time" (1 Peter 1:3-5).

We Hasten the Day!

Peter continues in 1 Peter 1:6-9 by pointing out that we rejoice in this hope, even though for a time we might suffer trials for the cause of Christ. Our faith can be shown genuine, and this will result "in praise and glory and honor at the revelation of Jesus Christ." Even though we do not see Jesus now, we believe and we rejoice because, in the end, we will obtain salvation. Hasten that day!

May we all live in such a way that we can say, with John, "Come, Lord Jesus" (Revelation 22:20).

Are you ready?

1. How should we act knowing that the Lord is coming again?

2. What will you personally do in order to make sure you are ready for the Lord's return?

12. Appreciate the Holy Spirit

In his closing remarks to the church at Corinth, Paul wrote, "The grace of the Lord Jesus Christ and the love of God and the fellowship of the Holy Spirit be with you all" (2 Corinthians 13:14). Having fellowship with the Holy Spirit is vital. Yet there is much confusion about what that means and how the Holy Spirit functions in the life of a Christian. As we think about foundations, we must not neglect the significance of the Spirit. There is much about the Spirit that may be beyond the scope of what we can do here, but we can provide a foundational overview.

The Holy Spirit is divine and personal.

The Spirit is not just some undefined "force" that is better felt than told. He is not a nebulous "it" with no personality or will. Rather, the Holy Spirit is God as much as the Father and the Son, Jesus Christ. The Spirit can "guide," "speak," and "declare" truth (John 16:13; 1 Timothy 4:1). He can bear witness (John 15:16), search hearts, and make intercession on behalf of others (Romans 8:26; 1 Corinthians 2:10). He can even forbid (Acts 16:6). The personal nature of the Spirit can be seen in Acts 13:2, when He said, "Set apart for *me* Barnabas and Saul…" The Scriptures present the Holy Spirit in a personal way.

The Holy Spirit also has divine attributes, just as the Father and the Son. The Spirit is all-knowing and can search all things, "even the depths of God" (1 Corinthians 2:10). Hebrews 9:14 refers to Him as the "eternal Spirit." All things are before Him and nothing is out of His sight (Psalm 139:7). He can even be lied to. In a passage that explicitly identifies the Spirit with God, we find a man named Ananias lying about money given. The apostle Peter told him,

"Satan filled your heart to lie to the Holy Spirit" (Acts 5:3). In the very next verse, Peter tells him, "You have not lied to man but to God" (v. 4). The Spirit can even be grieved by rebellion against Him (Isaiah 63:10; Ephesians 4:30). We will say more about that.

The point is that the Holy Spirit is divine and personal, and when we have fellowship with Him, we are having fellowship with God. We hope to develop a better appreciation for this.

The Holy Spirit is active throughout Scripture.

The Bible opens with these words: "In the beginning, God created the heavens and the earth. The earth was without form and void, and darkness was over the face of the deep. And the Spirit of God was hovering over the face of the waters" (Genesis 1:1-2).

The Spirit was active in the creation, just as Jesus was (John 1:1-4). The Spirit powerfully worked in the creation and shaping of the world. Later, we find the Spirit active in the exodus event when Israel left Egypt. God's presence was with the people, and this is said to be the presence of the Spirit. God put His Holy Spirit in their midst and the Spirit led them and gave them rest. Yet because of their rebellion, the people grieved the Spirit (read Isaiah 63:10-14).

The Spirit was also active in the revealing of God's word to the prophets. Of this time-frame, Peter writes that "men spoke from God as they were carried along by the Holy Spirit" (2 Peter 1:21). Jesus, speaking of David writing Psalm 110, said that David declared these things "in the Holy Spirit" (Mark 12:36). These are ways of saying that the Holy Spirit inspired these men to write. Many more passages can testify to this idea. The Holy Spirit was at work through the revealing of the word of God.

The Holy Spirit is also seen in the miraculous activities and spiritual gifts throughout Scripture. For example, the word of God, revealed by the Holy Spirit, would often then be confirmed by miraculous activity as proof that the message was from God. The Hebrews writer refers to this by saying, "God also bore witness by signs and wonders and various miracles and by gifts of the Holy Spirit distributed according to his will" (Hebrews 2:4). Even in the life of Christ, the Spirit is fully active. Peter spoke of "how God anointed Jesus of Nazareth with the Holy Spirit and with power. He went about doing good and healing all who were oppressed by the devil, for God was with him" (Acts 10:38). Jesus was attested by God "with mighty works and wonders and signs that God did through him" (Acts 2:22). Jesus said that He cast out demons "by the Spirit of God" (Matthew 12:28). In the parallel of this, the Spirit is referred to as "the finger of God" (Luke 11:20). Since the Father, Son, and Holy Spirit are divine, the working together in complete unity should not surprise us.

Jesus promised His chosen disciples that the Spirit would come upon them and deliver all truth (John 16:12-13). They were to receive the power of the Spirit as they embarked upon their role after Jesus had ascended to heaven (Acts 1:8). The book of Acts shows how some of this occurred in the lives of some of the apostles. Yet there is more to be seen for all believers.

1. Why is understanding the Holy Spirit as divine and personal so important?

2. How active is the Holy Spirit throughout Scripture? What are some of the actions we see Him doing?

The Holy Spirit is present for the believer.

When Peter preached on Pentecost in Acts 2, he preached, "Repent and be baptized every one of you in the name of Jesus Christ for the forgiveness of your sins, and you will receive the gift of the Holy Spirit" (v. 38). He then said that this was a promise "for your children and for all who are far off, everyone whom the Lord our God calls to himself" (v. 39). While the "gift of the Holy Spirit" can be a controversial phrase, we want to stress something very simple here. This is a promise that God's presence would be with Christians. What this also means is that we do have fellowship of the Holy Spirit in our walk as God's children.

In the garden, Adam and Eve were in the presence of the Lord. They had rest. When they sinned, they lost their peace and they hid from God's presence (Genesis 3:18). When Cain sinned, He fled God's presence (Genesis 4:16).

Yet God's presence was given to the children of Israel through His Spirit, as Isaiah 63:7-14 shows us. God told Moses, "My presence shall go with you, and I will give you rest" (Exodus 33:14), and the Spirit fulfilled that role (Isaiah 63:14).

When they approached God's presence dishonorably, they suffered the consequences, as is seen in the account of Nabad and Abihu (Leviticus 10:2; 16:1). The bread in the tabernacle was called "the bread of His presence" (Numbers 4:7). Many other passages speak of God's presence, whether offering incense (Numbers 16:7), preparing for battle and crossing the Jordan (Numbers 32:29, 32), eating and the presentation of produce (Deuteronomy 14), the king writing a copy of the Law (Deuteronomy 17:18), and on we can go.

The essence of the gift of the Holy Spirit is the presence of God with us. What was lost in the garden (God's presence) is restored in Christ. The "presence of God" indicates God's walking in fellowship with His people. To think of the presence of God is to see His constant oversight, His care, and His willingness to be with and in

His people. When we are baptized into Christ, the Spirit is active in our new lives. "For in one Spirit we were all baptized into one body" (1 Corinthians 12:13). Paul affirmed that God saved us, "not because of works done by us in righteousness, but according to his own mercy, by the washing of regeneration and renewal of the Holy Spirit, whom he poured out on us richly through Jesus Christ our Savior" (Titus 2:5-6). This is in conjunction with being born through the word of God. Christians have been "born again, not of perishable seed but of imperishable, through the living and abiding word of God" (1 Peter 1:23). Remember that the Spirit is the revealer of God's mind (1 Corinthians 2:10-13). The word is His word, and it is living, active, powerful, and tied to God Himself (Hebrews 4:12-13).

Now the Holy Spirit is part of the Christian's life. Forgiveness and "times of refreshing" come from the presence of the Lord (Acts 3:19-20). God sets His seal on His people by the Holy Spirit who is given as a pledge of the full inheritance that we will one day receive (Ephesians 1:13-14). The Spirit is said to "dwell" in the child of God (Romans 8:9-11), indicating, again, a fellowship that results from God reconciling a sinner to Himself through Christ. This does not mean that all Christians have miraculous powers now. It means that God is with us, working in and through us, "to work for his good pleasure" (Philippians 2:12-13). The Spirit works with believers, for example, in their prayers, to intercede and help when we do not know how to pray as we ought (Romans 8:26-27). Though much of this will be beyond our ability to understand, we can trust the promises of God that He is active in our lives and for our benefit.

The presence of God through the Holy Spirit also helps us understand the church's role as God's temple, for His people are said to be "built together into a dwelling place for God by the Spirit" (Ephesians 2:22; see also 1 Corinthians 6:19 for individual

Christians). The picture of God's people follows the Old Testament temple picture. We are God's temple. We are God's priesthood offering up spiritual sacrifices (1 Peter 2:5, 9). The temple was about the presence of God among the people, and so now, God's presence is with His body of believers through the Spirit.

1. What is the essence of the gift of the Holy Spirit? Why does this matter to a Christian?

2. What Old Testament image is portrayed by the church as God's presence is found in His people?

The Holy Spirit leads us according to His word.

One of the ideas that we need to guard against is in thinking that the Holy Spirit is responsible for giving us certain feelings that make us think we can act certain ways. Scripture teaches, "For all who are led by the Spirit of God are sons of God" (Romans 8:14). Yet being led by the Spirit is not the idea that the Spirit is whispering in our ears or giving us feelings that make us think we can act as we desire. It would be wrong to attribute to the Spirit what the Spirit never claimed to do.

Being led by the Spirit is not about how we feel about something. If we are led by the Spirit, our feelings need to be brought under subjection to His revealed will. The Spirit has given us an objective standard by which we can know that we are following His lead. The context of Romans 8 is a contrast between walking by the flesh and walking by the Spirit. If we are truly being led by the Spirit, we will set our minds on the things of the Spirit (Romans 8:13). The "mind set on the Spirit" (v. 6) will never ignore what the Spirit has revealed, for that is the only way we will know the mind of God (1

Corinthians 2:10-13). The ones being led by the Spirit are the ones paying attention to His revelation. Feelings will follow, but letting our feelings take the lead can put us in that dangerous position of being led by the flesh instead of the Spirit.

This position is sometimes misunderstood for saying that the Spirit does nothing. On the contrary, we are recognizing that the Spirit not only works, but has so infused His revealed word with power that its impact will completely change us. The word works because the Spirit works, and the word is the Spirit's sword (Ephesians 6:17).

Read, again, Hebrews 4:12-13. God's word is living, active, powerful, sharp, and cuts to our very hearts. Why? Notice that verse 13 ties God into this message. The word is powerful because it is God's word. For the word to work, God must work. Scripture is not a lifeless piece of literature. What makes Scripture profitable for doctrine, reproof, correction, and instruction in righteousness is that it is inspired of God (2 Timothy 3:16-17). It is the message of the Spirit, who works in ways that we cannot fathom; He is able to do far more abundantly beyond anything we can ask or think (Ephesians 3:20). To deny the power of His word is to the deny the power of the Spirit to make His own communication do what He intends (Isaiah 55:8-11). Being led by the Spirit necessarily means that we are listening to this revealed message. No one who ignores Scripture can legitimately claim to be led by the Spirit.

Do not grieve the Holy Spirit.

Since the Spirit revealed God's mind, we are to pay close attention to this because it is possible that we might "drift away" from it (Hebrews 2:1-4). We cannot afford to turn away, for the Scriptures warn, "For it is impossible, in the case of those who have once been enlightened, who have tasted the heavenly gift, and have shared in the Holy Spirit, and have tasted the goodness of the word of God and the powers of the age to come, and then have fallen away, to restore them again to repentance, since they are crucifying once again the Son of God to their own harm and holding him up to contempt" (Hebrews 6:4-6). One who so turns away has a mindset that makes it impossible to please God. Those who turn away have "trampled underfoot the Son of God," "profaned the blood of the covenant by which he was sanctified, and has outraged the Spirit of grace" (Hebrews 10:29).

When the children of Israel rebelled, they grieved the Holy Spirit (Isaiah 63:10), and the apostle Paul warns against Christians doing the same (Ephesians 4:30). God has given us His Spirit, but if we turn away and rebel, we will grieve Him. If we maintain a rebellious mindset, repentance will be impossible. If, on the other hand, we repent and turn back to God, we can once again find comfort and forgiveness. Then, we can pray as did David, "Cast me not away from your presence, and take not your Holy Spirit from me" (Psalm 51:11).

The presence of God through the Spirit is a great comfort to us as His children. Let us, therefore, pay close attention to His revealed mind and set our minds on the things of the Spirit, for "anyone who does not have the Spirit of Christ does not belong to him" (Romans 8:9).

1. Why is it dangerous to assume that our feelings are being given to us by the Holy Spirit?

2. How can we grieve the Holy Spirit, and what can we do to guard against that?

13. Let Your Light Shine

Faith is meant to be lived. It is not some mere academic pursuit. It is not about the latest or best way to argue a point. It is about learning to trust and commit ourselves to our Lord. This is why the greatest apologetic will be your life — showing that God works in you and through you because you trust Him (Philippians 2:12ff).

Some "win" arguments through deceit, trickery, fallacy, or force. Others technically win arguments verbally, having carefully crafted solid reasons, yet no changes result. While it is important to know how to reason appropriately, and it never helps a cause to make bad arguments, the most important way to persuade another will always be through the lives that we live. Jesus taught that His disciples are to be lights in the world:

"You are the light of the world. A city set on a hill cannot be hidden. Nor do people light a lamp and put it under a basket, but on a stand, and it gives light to all in the house. In the same way, let your light shine before others, so that they may see your good works and give glory to your Father who is in heaven" (Matthew 5:14-16).

Paul wrote of Christians that they are to be lights or luminaries in a world that is twisted and crooked (Philippians 2:14 -16). Peter also wrote that Christians are to keep their behavior excellent so that others may observe their good works and ultimately glorify God (1 Peter 2:12).

Paul further wrote to Timothy, "And the Lord's servant must not be quarrelsome but kind to everyone, able to teach, patiently enduring evil, correcting his opponents with gentleness. God may perhaps grant them repentance leading to a knowledge of the truth, and they may come to their senses and escape from the snare of the devil, after being captured by him to do his will" (2 Timothy 2:24-26).

All of these passages have in common the idea that leading others to the Lord have much to do with our attitudes and the way we live our lives. Yet the reason we choose to live as we do is because we believe in God, His message, His grace, and His salvation through Jesus. Because we believe, we will live intentionally, striving to mirror God and His will. Here we want to be reminded of the importance of letting our lights shine in a dark world.

Our concern for others should be clear.

Standing up for Christ and defending His will should also have in mind evangelism (sharing the gospel). Souls are at stake in the fight for truth. Consequently, we are not just trying to win arguments and debates; we are trying to win souls for Christ. Therefore, *how* we converse with others is vital. Re-read 2 Timothy 2:24-26. The Lord's servant is not to be quarrelsome, but rather is to be kind, gentle, acting in such a way that he demonstrates the desire to bring others to Christ. We are to let our reasonable spirit be known to others (Philippians 4:5).

A humble spirit comes through as we take on the attitude of God, who is not willing that any should perish but that all should come to repentance (2 Peter 3:9). God's desire is that all be saved and come to the knowledge of the truth (1 Timothy 2:4). Further, if we have the mind of Christ (Philippians 2:5), then we will exhibit a spirit of sacrifice and selflessness.

When we approach the world with a sense of zeal, it can be easy to get caught up in the attitudes of trying to win arguments. We certainly ought to be enthusiastic in our efforts to reach others, but we also need to make sure that our focus stays on the goal of bringing people to Christ.

An approach bent on winning arguments for their own sakes is more geared toward glorifying the man, not God. A debate can be beneficial if done properly, but when we argue in ways that distort truth so that we can win a point, we overstep our boundaries. This is partly what Paul meant when he wrote the weapons of our warfare are not carnal (2 Corinthians 10:3-5). We must not stoop to worldly ways and ungodly methods in order to win points. That will only backfire on us. The weapons that God has given us are sufficient taking down the strongholds of the world and bringing every thought captive to Jesus Christ. We need to trust God in this.

Read 1 Timothy 2:3-4. If God's concern is the salvation of souls, then our concern ought to mirror this attitude. Jesus did not come to this earth to beat opponents in argumentation. He came to seek and save the lost. If we are going to honor Jesus for what He did, then our efforts should be directed toward those same goals. Taking an approach that places more emphasis on ourselves and upon our reasoning abilities ends up diminishing the honor that belongs to our Lord.

In all of our efforts to let our lights shine, we need to show our concern for others. This is about eternal life and death.

1. Why are our attitudes so important as we go into the world and try to stand up for Jesus?

2. Why is it important that others know you are truly concerned about them?

Live your life in Christ and stand up for Christ with grace.

The apostle Paul wrote, "Let your speech always be gracious, seasoned with salt, so that you may know how you ought to answer each person" (Colossians 4:6). What we say is extremely important. We cannot convert anyone to truth unless we actually speak the truth. Yet, Paul reminds us that *how* we go about it is just as important as the content of our message. Truth presented with a bad attitude or lack of kindness does no one any good. Truth is to be spoken in love (Ephesians 4:15) and with a desire to "give grace to those who hear" (Ephesians 4:29). Kindness is always in order when we are defending our Lord.

Further, we need to remember that part of the purpose in standing up for Jesus is to remove stumbling blocks and open doors. We do not want to slam doors by a bad attitude that turns people off to the message. If we get in the way of the message because we are not acting as we ought, then we are not glorifying God but ourselves. Therefore, in defending Jesus Christ (and all that goes with this) let us make sure we represent Him honorably so that glory goes to Him in all things. Once we have set apart Christ as Lord in our hearts, then we are in a position to give a defense of our hope, with gentleness and reverence (1 Peter 3:15).

Our job is to proclaim the excellencies of God (1 Peter 2:9-10) and to glorify Him in all that we do (1 Corinthians 10:31; cf. Colossians 3:17). Whatever good we may accomplish finds its value in glorifying God, not men. The Corinthians, who apparently put great stock in the wisdom of men, needed to learn this lesson. Paul indicated that even though the cross is foolishness to men, it is the power and wisdom of God through the cross that saves us from our sins. So when he preached to the Corinthians, he did not come to them "with superiority of speech or of wisdom." Rather, he was with them "in weakness and in fear and in much trembling." His message to them was not "in persuasive words of wisdom, but in demonstration of the Spirit and of power." Why? Paul's answer is straightforward: "so that your faith would not rest on the wisdom of men, but on the power of God" (1 Corinthians 2:1-5).

To defend Christ with grace means that we are kind in our approach, getting ourselves out of the way and giving all the glory to God. The power of God's word will hold its own. We need not embellish it or hide it. Let God's power shine through your presentation of His message.

Promote Christ with godly living.

Peter wrote that we must keep our behavior excellent among Gentiles (unbelievers), "so that when they speak against you as evildoers, they may see your good deeds and glorify God on the day of visitation" (1 Peter 2:12). This teaching coincides with what Jesus taught about His disciples being lights in the world (Matthew 5:16). While we recognize that we are far from perfect, we should understand that proclaiming allegiance to God on the one hand and living in a way that betrays this claim on the other hand will create stumbling blocks for others. The consequences of causing others to stumble are not good at all (cf. Matthew 18:6).

In order to live effectively for Christ, people must see beyond us to the Lord Himself. They need to know that it really is the Lord Christ whom we serve (Colossians 3:24). Therefore, we are to present ourselves to God as living and holy sacrifices (Romans 12:1) with the intent that we will not conform to the bad things of the world: "Do not be conformed to this world, but be transformed by the renewal of your mind, that by testing you may discern what is the will of God, what is good and acceptable and perfect" (Romans 12:2). Our duty to the world is to live like Christ and show His love and grace in a way that accurately reflects what God has done for us. We fail those in the world when we try to live like the world, and we fail God when we fail to follow His example.

Peter, also, reminds his readers of the need to be holy like God. "Prepare your minds for action," he wrote, with our hope fixed on the grace of Christ. We are to be "as obedient children" and "like the Holy One" who has called us. "You shall be holy, for I am holy" (1 Peter 1:13-16). To be holy is to be completely dedicated and set apart for God's service. It is to be focused on being like God as much as we can be. It is to shun evil things and focus on what is good and right as shown by the Lord. In this light, the best way to stand up for Christ in the world is by being holy and completely dedicated to God (with Christ set apart as Lord in the heart). This will promote Christ more than the words we might say. People need to know that we are different precisely because we are committed to Jesus as Lord.

Consequently, we will demonstrate our belief in God through the way that we love one another and show our unity in Him (John 13:34-35; John 17:20-21). Where the world shows hate, we will demonstrate love. Where the world expects retaliation, we will offer forgiveness. Where the world delights in sin, we will show our delight in godliness. We will abhor what is evil and cling to, and love, what is good (Romans 12:9). We will demonstrate God through holiness and desire to serve both God and others.

None of this means that we never have to say anything to others. The gospel message is found in words that need to be taught. However, the words alone are not what God is asking for. We must start with transformed lives, and then the words we speak to others will be truly meaningful.

1. Whose glory are we seeking when we stand up for Christ in this world? Why is that focus so vital?

2. What does it mean to be holy? Why should we seek to be holy?

Make the most of opportunities.

Paul wrote to the Colossians that we are not only to speak with grace, but we are to be "making the best use of the time" (Colossians 4:5). We are to walk carefully, "making the best use of the time, because the days are evil." (Ephesians 5:15-16). Once we have set apart Christ in our hearts as Lord and are striving to live holy lives, we should be looking for opportunities to act for the good of others. God's people have been redeemed (bought back out of sin) and purified so that they can be God's special possession, "zealous for good deeds" (Titus 2:14).

"And let us not grow weary of doing good, for in due season we will reap, if we do not give up. So then, as we have opportunity, let us do good to everyone, and especially to those who are of the household of faith" (Galatians 6:9-10). There may be times when it seems that our efforts are not going anywhere. Perhaps as we deal with people who have questions and doubts, we may feel that our discussions fall on deaf ears. The process can get old when it seems that no one is paying attention. Hang in there, Paul says. We will reap the reward for patience in the end.

Why is doing good for others important for taking the message of Christ to the world? Because this is what will help open doors for further study. People can see that you are serious about what you claim to believe. You are a helper, looking for ways to be a blessing and benefit to others. You are the one who consistently and proverbially (and literally) helps the older lady cross the street. You are the "Good Samaritan" of the parable in Luke 10, not one of the ones who pass by on the other side when someone is truly in need. People will know that you care, and when they know this, they will care more about what you have to offer. Just look for opportunities to help. Be a blessing, and it may surprise you who might be willing to listen as you speak of Jesus.

Get Ready to answer.

When you are living like you should in Christ and finding ways to help others and do good for them, make sure you are ready because sooner or later the questions will likely come. Once again, Peter wrote that Christians must be "ready to give a defense" for the reason of the hope within them (1 Peter 3:15). They may want to know why you live the way that you do? Why are you so sacrificial? Why do you go out of your way to serve others? Why did you engage in that act of kindness? Whatever the particular questions, the point is that you are ready to defend your faith and the hope that you have. You should not be terribly surprised when people want to know about it.

Never underestimate the value of living a godly life in defending the faith. Let your own life serve as an example to the world. May God bless you as you go out into the world and stand for Him.

1. How can doing good things for others open up opportunities to teach them the gospel?

2. Why should you be ready to give some answers about your hope? How can you do this?

Basic Glossary

Abraham: Abraham (first known as Abram) was called by God to be the one through whom God would carry out special promises that would ultimately result in salvation from sin. In Genesis 12, God promised Abraham that his descendants (sometimes called "seed") would become a special nation (whom we later know as Israel), that they would have a special (Palestine or Canaan), and they through his "seed" all the families of the earth would be blessed. This blessing promise was meant to finally be fulfilled in Jesus Christ, and the blessing would be the forgiveness of sins (see Acts 3:24-26). Abraham's faith is exemplary, having believed God and His promises and acting in a way that showed how much he trusted God. This kind of faith is held up for Christians to imitate (Romans 4:16-25).

Adam and Eve: the first pair of human beings. God created the heavens and the earth, and on day six He created Adam and Eve as male and female. He created them in His image (Genesis 1:26-27). He put them in a garden we know as Eden and expected them to tend and keep it (Genesis 2:15). There was one restriction, however, and this that they could eat of every tree in the garden but one known as the tree of the knowledge of good and evil. Satan, the adversary of God and His people, appeared as a serpent and tempted Eve in particular to eat of the forbidden fruit. She did eat and gave some to Adam who was with her (Genesis 3:1-5). This sin by Adam and Eve set off a series of consequences that affect not only them but all of creation. Corruption and death entered the world at that point and the problem of sin became a problem from that time forward. Only God would be able to offer the solution to save human beings from the problem of sin. This plan was immediately put into effect (Genesis 3:15).

Angel: a messenger. In a special sense, angels are known to be spiritual beings who are supposed to work on God's behalf and for God's people. They were involved in carrying messages to God's people and would sometimes appear in more human form. For example, when Jesus' mother, Mary, was chosen to be Jesus' mother, an angel delivered the message to her and also to Joseph, who would be Mary's husband (Matthew 1:18-25; Luke 1:26-38).

Apostle: "one sent." An apostle was technically someone who was sent by another on a special mission. Those whom we know as apostles in the New Testament are those specially chosen by Jesus Christ to carry out the mission He began. He initially chose twelve men to be apostles and gave them special authority to teach, heal, and cast out demons (Matthew 10:1-15). Later, a man named Saul, who become known as Paul, was specially chosen to be an apostle (Acts 9; 1 Corinthians 15:1-8). One of the requirements was that the man so chosen was a witness of the resurrected Jesus (see Acts 1:21-26).

Baptism: in the New Testament, baptism refers to immersion. When one is baptized into Christ, that one is immersed in water, which connects that person to the death, burial, and resurrection of Jesus Christ (Romans 6:3-5). That person is then raised up to walk in newness of life. In Acts 2, Peter told the people, "Repent and be baptized every one of you in the name of Jesus Christ for the forgiveness of your sins, and you will receive the gift of the Holy Spirit" (v. 38). While baptism is not about cleansing the physical body, it is about making an appeal to God for a good conscience (1 Peter 3:20-21).

Bible: see the chapter *Meet the Bible*. The Bible is the collection of sixty-six books also known as Scripture. It consists of thirty-nine books in the Old Testament and twenty-seven books in the New Testament. The Bible was written by over forty human authors over a period of 1,500-1,600 years. However, the Bible comes together in a way that believers accept it as the inspired word of God, which is profitable for all our teaching and is able to give us the wisdom to be saved from our sins (2 Timothy 3:15-16).

Christ: the New Testament term for "anointed." Jesus is called the Christ, meaning that He is the One who was anointed by God to be His special King. The Old Testament counterpart is the term "Messiah." "Christ," then, is not the last name of Jesus, but rather describes who He is.

Church: see the chapters *Know the Church* parts 1 and 2. The word church (*ekklesia*) in the New Testament is a term that basically refers to a group or assembly of people. It could refer to any group or gathering of people (as in Acts 19). The term was then used to refer to God's group or collection of people. "Church" can refer universally to all of God's people, regardless of when or where they are. It can also refer to a local group of people assembled together. Those who are in Christ's church are those whose names are enrolled in heaven (Hebrews 12:23).

David: a specifically chosen king of Israel and Judah. He was the second king of Israel before the nation officially divided into north (Israel) and south (Judah). David was chosen by God, and even though he had some very personal problems to deal with, overall he was considered to be a man after God's own heart (Acts 13:22). David became the standard for the kings, and his kingship is used as the pattern after which Jesus Christ would follow. Jesus would be raised up to sit on David's throne and rule over His own kingdom. While this rule is not like normal earthly kingdoms, it was part of God's plan to establish His special kingdom under Jesus Christ.

Demon: a spiritual creature who essentially works for the devil or Satan. The assumption is usually that demons were possibly angels who decided to rebel against God and join with the rebellion of the Satan. They, along with Satan, will be judged and confined to hell (Matthew 25:41).

Disciple: a disciple is a learner or follower of another. We often read of the disciples of Jesus, which simply means that these are people who learned from and followed the teachings of Jesus and His apostles. Christians today are also known as disciples of Christ.

Faith: biblical faith is trust. While faith involves believing in God, it is more than mere mental agreement with something. Faith translates into action because when one trusts God, that one will seek to do God's will. Without faith, one cannot please God (Hebrews 11:6). Faith demonstrates one's convictions that God is real, what God says is true, and that God can be completely trusted. Faith will then act consistently with that conviction.

Fellowship: this means a joint participation in something special. People have a normal type of fellowship when they do things together, such as eating or working. Christians have a special fellowship with God and with each other through their common relationship with Jesus Christ. Sin can break that fellowship, but forgiveness will bring enemies back together again. Fellowship in Christ is special for God's people as they join together to serve the Lord and encourage each other in their efforts.

Grace: see the chapter *Cherish Salvation by Grace*. Because sin breaks fellowship with God, we are not in a position to be able to fix that problem on our own. God is the One who must bring the solution, and the solution is what we know as grace. This is God's kindness and mercy toward us in offering us a way back to full fellowship with Him through having our sins forgiven. We do not deserve such kindness from God, but He offers it because He loves us. Grace, then, is God given us what we do not deserve and can never earn, namely forgiveness and fellowship. Without God's grace, there can be no salvation from sin.

Israel: this name refers to the people who descended from Abraham and became God's specially chosen nation through whom He would carry out the promises that would lead to salvation through Jesus Christ. Where did the name come from? Abraham had a son named Isaac, and Isaac had a son named Jacob. Jacob, though many difficulties, was given the name Israel by God (Genesis 32:27-28). Jacob, in turn, had twelve sons, and these with their families became known as the children of Israel. Those who descended from Israel were the ones who went down to Egypt, became slaves, and were later set free by Moses and brought into a covenant relationship with God.

Kingdom: refers primarily to the rule or reign of God over all others. When we think of earthly kingdoms, we think of kings and subjects over which the king rules. In the New Testament, the kingdom of God was set up under the rule of Jesus Christ, who was raised from the dead to sit on David's throne. This indicates that Christ's kingdom is His rule in a special sense. Jesus would not be like a typical earthly king, for His kingdom is not of this world and His servants do not fight like would be done in an earthly kingdom (John 18:36). While Christ is King over all the world and has the power to judge, there is a special sense in which He rules over His own people who have been "delivered us from the domain of darkness and transferred us to the kingdom of his beloved Son, in whom we have redemption, the forgiveness of sins" (Colossians 1:13-14).

Moses: Moses was born when the people of Israel were being worked as slaves in Egypt. He was born to a Hebrew family, but because the Pharaoh, Egypt's king, was putting Hebrew babies to death, Moses' mother hid him and put him in a basket in the river. Moses was found by Pharaoh's daughter and raised as an Egyptian, while also learning the ways of the Hebrews (Israel). He grew up and had to flee from Egypt for a time, but he was later called by God to go back to Egypt and tell Pharaoh to let the people of Israel go. When Pharaoh refused, God unleashed a series of plagues on Egypt, but spared the people of Israel. Moses was finally able to bring them out of Egypt, cross the Red Sea, bring them to a place called Mt. Sinai, and there receive the Law from God to deliver to the people. For forty years Moses led the people in the wilderness south of the land of Palestine. He brought the people to the edge of the promised land where he would die. Joshua, Moses' successor, would be the one who led the people into the land.

Repentance: this is a deliberate act of turning one's life around. Repentance begins in the mind and heart, where one determines that he cannot keep living in rebellion against God. He then determines to turn to God and strive to live in a way that is consistent with what God's word teaches.

Satan: means "adversary." Satan is also known as the devil, which means "slanderer." The devil was a created being who had considerable power, but chose at some point to rebel against God.

He became the adversary to God and God's people. In doing so, he also became one who slandered God and makes false accusations against the people of God. However, he is not all-powerful, and Scripture shows that God finally judges the devil and confines him to hell (Matthew 25:41). Christians are taught to be careful about the schemes of the devil (Ephesians 6:11). While the devil cannot make anyone do wrong, he has the ability to present temptations in a way that are deceiving. The apostle Peter says, "Be sober-minded; be watchful. Your adversary the devil prowls around like a roaring lion, seeking someone to devour. Resist him, firm in your faith..." (1 Peter 5:8-9). According to James, the Lord's brother, if we will submit ourselves to God and resist the devil, "will flee from you" (James 4:7).

Paul: first known as Saul of Tarsus in the New Testament. Saul first persecuted Christians and very much opposed Christ and His followers. He was causing all kinds of problems for them until, one day, Christ appeared to him and Saul was converted (Acts 9). Saul later became known as the apostle Paul, and the latter part of the book of Acts is devoted to his travels as he tried to preach Christ. Paul also wrote a number of the New Testament books known as epistles (letters) to various churches and individuals. These include Romans, 1 and 2 Corinthians, Galatians, Ephesians, Philippians, Colossians, 1 and 2 Thessalonians, 1 and 2 Timothy, Titus, and Philemon.

Peter: one of the original twelve apostles, Peter stands out as one of the more prominent disciples of Jesus and leader in the early church in the New Testament. He is known for his great confession of Jesus as the Christ, the Son of the Living God (Matthew 16:13-20), but also sometimes for being a bit impetuous (see John 18:10-11). While, sadly, Peter denied Jesus when Jesus was on trial, he repented and become a great leader among God's people. The first several chapters of Acts focus on much of what Peter did, and Peter is responsible for writing 1 and 2 Peter in the New Testament.

Prophet: a mouthpiece for God. A true prophet of God was called by God to speak His message. The Holy Spirit would inspire the prophet to speak God's message to the people. The prophets in the Old Testament spoke to the people at a time when the people were straying from God and His will. They called the people back to God, rebuking them for idolatry, injustices, and mere ritualism, so that they could avert judgment. Sadly, the people, for the most part, did not listen to the prophets. Yet the prophets also pointed ahead to the time that Jesus Christ would come and fulfill the plan of God. For instance, the prophets often spoke about that which later would be fulfilled by Jesus Christ (for example, see Isaiah 53).

Salvation: in Scripture, salvation might come in different forms. For example, someone might be saved from a destruction of a city, like Lot was saved or rescued from the destruction of Sodom (Genesis 19). But salvation is much more than that when it comes to salvation from sin. God offers salvation from sin through Jesus Christ, who died for our sins and rose again from the dead. Salvation, then, indicates that we are freed and rescued from sin and its consequence of ultimate death (Romans 6:23). God rescues us from what our sins will do to us, by His grace, and give us the hope of eternal life with Him. We are saved by the blood of Jesus, saved by the grace of God, and saved to be with Him forever!

Sin: sin is a violation of God's will. God has made His will known for how people ought to behave. He has also given human beings the free will to act as they wish, though He desires that everyone submit to His will. When we do what we want instead of what God wants, we fall short of God's glory and are guilty of sin (Romans 3:23). Because sin is a such a terrible violation of God and His holy character, the consequences result in death. This initially means that we are separated from the fellowship of God. However, because God wants fellowship with those whom He has created, He initiated a plan through which we can be reconciled to Him and brought back into His fellowship. This plan was that Jesus Christ, who Himself is God, would come in the flesh and die for our sins. Then He would be raised from the dead and show that He has defeated death. This means then that God, by His grace, would offer forgiveness for sin and a renewed fellowship for believers. This also means that believers have a hope for their own resurrection and eternal life with God.

Basic Bible Timeline

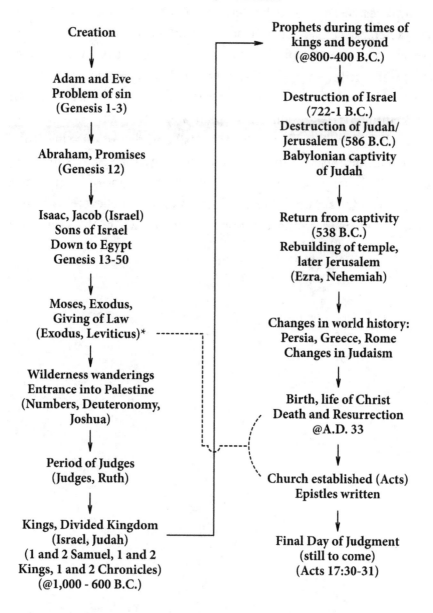

Creation
↓
Adam and Eve
Problem of sin
(Genesis 1-3)
↓
Abraham, Promises
(Genesis 12)
↓
Isaac, Jacob (Israel)
Sons of Israel
Down to Egypt
Genesis 13-50
↓
Moses, Exodus,
Giving of Law
(Exodus, Leviticus)*
↓
Wilderness wanderings
Entrance into Palestine
(Numbers, Deuteronomy,
Joshua)
↓
Period of Judges
(Judges, Ruth)
↓
Kings, Divided Kingdom
(Israel, Judah)
(1 and 2 Samuel, 1 and 2
Kings, 1 and 2 Chronicles)
(@1,000 - 600 B.C.)

Prophets during times of
kings and beyond
(@800-400 B.C.)
↓
Destruction of Israel
(722-1 B.C.)
Destruction of Judah/
Jerusalem (586 B.C.)
Babylonian captivity
of Judah
↓
Return from captivity
(538 B.C.)
Rebuilding of temple,
later Jerusalem
(Ezra, Nehemiah)
↓
Changes in world history:
Persia, Greece, Rome
Changes in Judaism
↓
Birth, life of Christ
Death and Resurrection
@A.D. 33
↓
Church established (Acts)
Epistles written
↓
Final Day of Judgment
(still to come)
(Acts 17:30-31)

*The Law of Moses was intended to bring the people to Jesus. Once fulfilled in Christ, it was no longer to be bound (Galatians 3:23-26). A new covenant was established (Hebrews 8:8-13; Jeremiah 31:31-34).

Synopses of Bible Books

Old Testament Books
The Jews saw these books divided into three sections: the Law, the Prophets, and the Writings. This is also called the *TaNaKh*, which is an acronym for the *Torah* (the Law), the *Nevi'im* (Prophets), and the *Ketuvim* (Writings). Jesus said that "all that was written about Him in the Law, the Prophets, and the Psalms must be fulfilled" (Luke 24:44-45). This fits the same three-fold designation of this part of Scripture:

Genesis
The book of beginnings: Creation of heavens and earth, plants, animals, and mankind. Sin brings curse upon creation, and mankind is separated from God. God puts into effect His plan for mankind's redemption and salvation. He gives the promise to Abram (then Isaac and Jacob) that through his seed, all nations would be blessed. This would ultimately be fulfilled in Jesus Christ. The book shows the start of how God would bring this plan into effect.

Exodus
The children of Israel (Jacob) had become slaves in Egypt. God chose Moses to lead the people out of Egypt so that they could be His special nation through which Messianic promises (the seed promise given to Abraham) could be fulfilled. After much turmoil with Pharaoh and the plagues God brought upon them, the children of Israel finally left Egypt and received the Law at Mt. Sinai. Various laws, the Passover, and the tabernacle (God's "dwelling" among the people) receive special attention. God's mighty acts of power are stressed.

Leviticus

A book pertaining primarily to the work of the Levites and the Priesthood. It deals with the various responsibilities of the priests, particularly regarding the sacrifices (worship) and their holiness (living as God's people should live). Perhaps the key passage is in 11:44-45, where God stated, "be holy, for I am holy." Peter quoted from this, showing how Christians are to be holy themselves (1 Peter 1:15-16). Holiness is the theme.

Numbers

"Numbers" (census) refers to the counting of the Israelites. In the book, the children of Israel continued their *wilderness wanderings*. Due to their complaints, the older generation of Israel would die in the wilderness, unable to enter the promised land (chapters 13-14). The younger generation is then prepared for entering the land. Throughout the book are seen the consequences of disbelief and disobedience.

Deuteronomy

Deuteronomy is the repetition of the law given at Sinai. At the end of Moses' life, he gave the children of Israel this last series of addresses in which he reiterated the need to obey God and remain faithful to God's covenant. Commandments and warnings are given throughout, with the respective blessings and curses. Obedience would result in continued favor from God; disobedience would result in the loss of special blessings.

Joshua

After Moses died, Joshua became the leader of the children of Israel. Under his leadership, they entered the promised land of Canaan and conquered it. The land was then divided into sections for the habitation of the tribes. At the end of his life, Joshua encouraged the people to choose to serve the Lord continually. The people were faithful to God as long as Joshua was alive.

Judges

After entering and dividing the land, the people went through cycles in which they engaged in sin. God would then allow some oppressors to give them problems. After their cries for help, God would send deliverers (judges) to save them from the bad situation. This would be followed by a period of peace. Then they would enter the cycle of sin again. Judges 2 shows how the cycle continued to get worse and spiral downward as Israel remained unfaithful to the covenant.

Ruth

Ruth was a Moabite woman who had married into an Israelite family, in the days of the judges. When her husband died, she determined to return to Israel with her mother-in-law, Naomi, and worship Yahweh. She went to work in the field of Boaz. Boaz redeemed her (see ch. 4), and they were eventually married. They were ancestors of Jesus. The story is one of love, devotion, and reward, with a primary point showing how the seed promise would continue in David's line.

1 Samuel

Samuel was the last of the judges. He was a righteous man. But the people were not satisfied with what they had and asked for a king so they could like the nations around them. God would let this happen, but they would soon find out that having kings was not going to be so great for them. Saul was the first king. He turned out to be wicked, and David was chosen by God to take over as king when Saul died. 1 Samuel focuses on the reigns of Saul and David, contrasting the two men as one turned from God (Saul) and the other turned toward God (David).

2 Samuel

2 Samuel zeros in on the reign of David and the difficulties he faced as king, as well as the consequences of his own sins. His sin with Bathsheba, the rebellion and death of Absalom his son, and the

other struggles he faced are found here. We also see David's ultimate desire to do what is right in the sight of God. In spite of the problems, God promised David that his seed would establish a kingdom forever (2 Samuel 7:12-13).

1 Kings

1 Kings deals with the final years of David as king of Israel, the reign of Solomon (David's son), and begins the narrative of the divided kingdom years (the northern kingdom is still called Israel; the southern kingdom is called Judah). It is the story of a great nation which had a glorious beginning, but fell into a terrible state of apostasy. After Solomon, the kingdom divided, and the majority of those who were God's people fell into such sin that they would eventually be punished for it.

2 Kings

2 Kings continues where 1 Kings ends. After the kingdom of Israel divided, the kings of the northern kingdom of Israel became increasingly wicked. They were finally carried away by the Assyrians in about 721 B.C. Meanwhile, Judah lasted longer, but still would eventually fall as captives to the Babylonians. This book shows how God removed kings and carried out the covenant curses (from Deuteronomy) against those who disobeyed Him.

1 Chronicles

1 Chronicles has several parallels to what is also covered in later 1 Samuel and much of 2 Samuel. It contains much genealogical information in the first several chapters. The book primarily covers the reigns of Saul and David. It appears to have been written after Babylonian exile to remind the people how unfaithfulness to God yields bad results (see chapter 9:1—"Judah was carried away into exile to Babylon for their unfaithfulness.").

2 Chronicles

2 Chronicles continues where 1Chronicles leaves off. Solomon is king over all Israel, and is now going to build the temple for which David had helped make preparations before he died. Building the temple is successful. However, after Solomon died, Rehoboam, his son, took over, and the kingdom soon split. It ends with the sad events of Judah being carried away to captivity and the destruction of Jerusalem (about 586 B.C.).

Ezra

As the prophets foretold, the people of God went into captivity for 70 years in Babylon due to their unfaithfulness. After this time, Cyrus, king of Persia, was stirred up to allow them to go back home and rebuild their temple (about 538 B.C.). A remnant returned to Jerusalem to build the temple (finished in 516 B.C.), and later the walls of the city of Jerusalem (444 B.C.). Ezra records what happened as they returned from captivity. He was active in calling the people back to God. Ezra's return was in about 458 B.C.

Nehemiah

Though earlier Jews had returned from exile and rebuilt the temple (Ezra), the walls of the city of Jerusalem were still in ruins. When Nehemiah heard of this, he wept, prayed, and asked to be able to return to complete this task. He was allowed to do so, and under great pressure from without, he led the rebuilding of the walls. It was completed in 52 days because the people had a mind to work together. This was in about the year 444 B.C.

Esther

Ezra speaks of the return of Zerubbabel to rebuild the temple (about 536 B.C.). Nehemiah covers his own return to rebuild the city (about 444 B.C.). Esther falls in between (about 483 B.C.). She was a Jewess who was crowned Queen of Persia. During her time, an effort was made to destroy all Jews. Because of her willingness and efforts, the people were saved. Though God's name is not mentioned, the book plays a vital, historical role in the fulfillment of God's plan as His people are spared from destruction.

Job

Job was a righteous man whom God allowed Satan to test. He lost his children and possessions, and suffered tremendous physical pain. Three friends visited Job, and began to accuse him of sin. Job defended himself, but God finally spoke and showed how they all were thinking wrongly about matters. In the end, Job was blessed even more than he had been before. He remained faithful throughout his sufferings. Trusting God through difficulties and trials is the theme.

Psalms

Basically, a psalm is a special song of praise. The Psalms are a collection of songs and poetry, covering many different moods and feelings. There is much praise for God, and they contain some of the deep feelings that the writers themselves had as they were struggling through their times. Many were written by David, though there were several other authors involved.

Proverbs

A proverb is a general saying that teaches practical wisdom. The book of Proverbs is a collection of such sayings setting forth godly wisdom. Solomon is the chief human author, but others were also involved. A host of subjects are treated, and the wisdom set forth is timeless for all ages. It is important for us to be familiar with the book today, as the applications are always needed for making choices in life that glorify God. The foundation for godly wisdom and knowledge is the fear of the Lord (Proverbs 1:7).

Ecclesiastes

The one called Koheleth (the "preacher") sought to find meaning to life through many avenues such as wisdom, pleasure, riches, and power, all apart from God. He kept coming up empty: "all is vanity."

The things of life are fleeting and empty, especially when one tries to live without God. True meaning in life is found in serving God. The conclusion, after all was heard, was to fear God and keep His commandments. God will bring every act to judgment, so life "under the sun" is all about serving Him.

Song of Solomon

This is love poetry expressing a man's desire for a special woman. The song shows the importance of the physical aspect of love within marriage. God created the physical union between husband and wife for mutual enjoyment, but God still expects us to show wisdom and purity. Many have used the book allegorically for God's relationship to Israel, or even Christ's relationship to the church. The primary point, however, is about the love within marriage.

A Note on the Prophets: the prophets were God's mouthpieces to the people during difficult and strained times. They generally operated between about 800 B.C. and 400 B.C. They pointed the people back to the Covenant God made with them. They called out common sins of which the people needed to repent, primarily the sins of idolatry, religious ritualism (just going through motions while living sinful lives), and oppression of the poor and needy. They also pointed to the Messiah (Jesus Christ). Through the prophets, God gave the people many opportunities to return to Him. Sadly, most of the people did not listen.

Isaiah

Isaiah prophesied beginning at the end of the reign of King Uzziah (6:1), from about 740-700 B.C.. He gave many warnings to Israel, and was around to witness Isreal's demise. He also worked with Hezekiah of Judah. But Isaiah is usually most noted for the Messianic prophecies contained throughout the Book. He is quoted in the New Testament more than any other prophet.

Jeremiah

Jeremiah prophesied during the time that Judah was taken away into captivity, and the city of Jerusalem was destroyed. He warned Judah that if they did not repent, they would be just like their sister Israel. He endured a great deal of suffering in order to preach to the people, even though few listened. He is sometimes referred to as the "weeping" prophet because of his sorrow over the nation.

Lamentations

Lamentations, written by Jeremiah the prophet, is a dirge of mourning over Jerusalem. Written after the fall of Jerusalem in 586 B.C., the prophet mourns over the desolation of the city. It is, essentially, the funeral of Jerusalem. It was used by the Jews as a reminder of the consequences of sin. Even so, they are also reminded of the faithfulness of God who would allow them to return.

Ezekiel

Ezekiel was one of the Israelites taken in captivity by the Babylonians. He was a priest who received visions and revelations from God about the nations, Israel's restoration, and the temple. He reminded the people why they were in captivity, but his message was ultimately one of hope to the common people. The book is filled with figures that help the message come to life.

Daniel

Daniel was a young man taken into captivity by the Babylonians to serve the King, Nebuchadnezzar. God gave him the ability to interpret dreams and prophesy. He foretold the history of the nations after Babylon, and how the kingdom of God would be established to overcome them all. There are great lessons about what it means to be faithful to God, even in difficult times.

Hosea

Hosea's message is to the northern kingdom of Israel before she fell. God had begged her to return to Him, but she kept committing spiritual adultery against God. One sees the heart of God bleeding as He yearns for Israel to return to Him. As an object lesson, Hosea married a woman who committed adultery against him; then he was told to take her back. This showed God's love toward Israel as He continued to take her back after sinning against Him.

Joel

Joel's message was one of calling God's people back to Him in light of approaching judgment. He uses a terrible plague of locusts to foretell judgment. He also has Messianic implications, as is seen in the fact that Peter quotes from Joel 2 on the day of Pentecost (Acts 2), and preaches that what Joel said was fulfilled.

Amos

Amos prophesied in the eighth century B.C. to Israel, during a time of wealth and corruption. He strongly condemned their addictions to luxury, idolatry, and moral depravity. Because of these things, they would go into captivity. Amos emphasizes the character of God and His relation to the nation.

Jonah

Jonah was sent by God to the Ninevites (capital of Assyria) to tell them of their impending destruction. At first Jonah ran from it, but after three days in the belly of a fish, he went when God told him to go again. When he preached, they repented, and God did not destroy them just yet. This angered Jonah, and he was rebuked for his attitude. It shows God's care for the lost. Jesus used Jonah's account to foretell His resurrection (Matthew 12:40).

Micah

Micah was contemporary with Isaiah, prophesying to "Samaria and Jerusalem" (the northern and southern capital cities). His effort was to remind rebellious people that "the Lord is coming forth from His place." They will be judged for their sins. Yet Micah also has prophecies about the Christ. God would spare a remnant, in which His plans would be fulfilled.

Nahum

Like Jonah, Nahum was a prophet to Ninevah. However, this time, Ninevah, the capital of Assyria, would not be spared. So Nahum prophesied shortly before the fall of Assyria in about 612 B.C. His theme is very pointed: it is about the fall and destruction of Ninevah. Once again, the lesson is taught that for a nation to survive, it must be established on the principles of righteousness and truth.

Habakkuk

Habakkuk prophesied from about 612-605 B.C., about the same time as Nahum and Jeremiah. He was concerned about the wickedness in the land, and wondered when God would do something about it. God told him that He would handle it in His time, using the Chaldeans (Babylonians) to punish Judah, then punishing Babylon for their own wickedness. One of the major themes is "wait on the Lord." Let God take care of matters in His own time.

Zephaniah

Zephaniah prophesied during the days of Josiah (c. 639-608 B.C.). Josiah's reign was preceded by Manasseh, whose wickedness sealed the destruction of Judah. However, Josiah stalled it by his great reforms; but Zephaniah still spoke of the Day of Jehovah, a day of judgment. Only a remnant would escape it. Yet, there would be a day of redemption. Further, Zephaniah emphasizes that Jehovah is the God of the universe. He is above all.

Haggai

Haggai returned from Babylonian captivity with those under Zerubbabel (starting at about 538 B.C.). Upon return, the people started rebuilding the temple, but then ceased. Haggai's message was very pointed: build the temple! The people needed to accomplish this task if they were to have the hope of blessing from God. The Messianic hope is seen in his message: the house would be filled with glory that would surpass anything else they had seen. The people did finally get back to work on the temple and finished it about 516 B.C.

Zechariah

Zechariah worked in conjunction with Haggai to urge the people to rebuild the temple. The background for their messages is identical. Zechariah's message was even more Messianic, looking beyond the material temple to the Messiah and His spiritual temple. God's purpose would be fulfilled through the Messiah and His rule. Even though there would be much opposition, God would fight for His people, and they would be victorious.

Malachi

Malachi was the last of the prophets prior to the 400 year span between the Old and New Testaments. The temple and the city had been rebuilt, but now the people had fallen into a state of indifference. Worship was in decay; they were divorcing their wives to marry heathens. Malachi makes it clear that their actions were intolerable to God. They needed to wake up and return to the Lord.

New Testament Books

A Note on the Gospels: Matthew, Mark, Luke, and John are referred to as the Gospels. These are snapshots of particular aspects of the life and teachings of Jesus Christ. Matthew, Mark, and Luke are very similar in nature and are sometimes called the synoptic Gospels because they are "seeing together" essentially the same events and teachings, though there are differences. John has his own unique style and emphasis. All four Gospels teach the death and resurrection of Jesus as the culmination of what He intended to accomplish.

Matthew

Matthew's focus is the kingship of Jesus. Jesus is presented as the Son of David who came to rule on His throne. Jesus is the promised Messiah (Christ, anointed one) and His works and miracles testified to this. Jesus died on a cross and was raised again, and through the resurrection secured His kingship. All authority thus belongs to Him.

Mark

Mark is written with a focus on showing that Jesus is the Christ, the Son of God (Mark 1:1). He emphasizes the miracles of Jesus to show that He is who He claimed to be. The first part of Mark ends with Peter confessing that Jesus is the Christ, and latter part shows that, as Jesus died, even a Roman centurion recognized that He is the Son of God. Mark's style is brief and to the point.

Luke

Luke began by claiming to have investigated everything carefully, including the eyewitnesses to Jesus, so that Theophilus, to whom Luke wrote, would know exactly what happened (Luke 1:1-4). Luke emphasizes the humanity of Jesus as He ministered to the poor, but also shows that He was indeed the promised Messiah who would bring salvation. Jesus came to seek and save the lost.

John

John's style differs much from the other writers. He emphasizes the divine nature of Jesus. Jesus is presented at the Creator, the Light of the world who brings life, and the Lamb of God who would die to take away the sins of the world. Jesus is God who came in the flesh (1:14), demonstrating His great love for us by going to the cross. In spite of the fact that Jesus is divine, He voluntarily subjected Himself to the suffering and death of the cross to bring salvation.

Acts

Acts was written by Luke as a "part 2" to Luke's Gospel. Jesus ascends to heaven after the resurrection and leaves the work of teaching the world to His chosen disciples. The apostles begin in Jerusalem and then start carrying the gospel message out to the ends of the world. The first part of Acts focuses on Peter, while the second part focuses on the apostle Paul after his conversion to Christ. Overarching all of this is the work of the Holy Spirit in confirming the message of the gospel as being the truth. Acts ends with Paul as a prisoner in Rome, but the implications are that the work of spreading the gospel had just begun.

Letters written by Paul (between @ A.D. 50-66)

Romans

The relationship between Jews and Gentiles (non-Jews) who became Christians was one of the early problems for disciples. Paul, here writing to a large Gentile audience, stressed the fact that both Jews and Gentiles were guilty of sin before God. Both Jews and Gentiles stood before God needing forgiveness and grace. The Jews could not simply appeal to the Law to be justified, nor could either group claim superiority over the other. All sinned and needed grace, and ultimately both groups must come together in Christ and respect each other's situations.

1 Corinthians

Corinth was at the crossroads of many philosophies and cultures. Because of this, it was known as a very immoral place. The church at Corinth was reflecting the problems of the culture and were struggling to stay united in Christ. Paul writes to plead with them to be united and to treat one another with love as they work through the issues that threatened them.

2 Corinthians

Paul had rebuked the Corinthians in the first letter, and now with one of them repenting of sin, they needed to learn how to show love and forgive. Paul also had his critics, and there were those who were trying to compete with Paul's authority, which forced Paul to defend his apostleship. Paul warns that they must not allow their focus on Christ to be divided.

Galatians

The problems between Jew and Gentile are dealt with head on. There were some Jewish teachers who were affirming that Gentiles, in order to be Christians, had first to be circumcised and essentially keep the Law of Moses. Paul wrote that they needed to guard against the perversion of the gospel message. In Christ, they were set free from the Law of Moses and needed to stay true to Jesus. The Law had served its purpose in bringing people to Christ.

Ephesians

Paul enumerates the blessings found in Christ. The first three chapters stress these blessings and the salvation from sin by grace through faith. Because of this, they were to strive to walk in a manner worthy of the calling from God. The last three chapters provide practical teachings about growing in Christ and living in the way that God desires. This includes being prepared to fight the spiritual battles that all Christians face.

Philippians

The church at Philippi had helped Paul in his preaching of the gospel. Paul writes to encourage them in their work and fellowship. They were to live properly, do nothing selfishly, treat others as more important than themselves, and show the mind of Christ in the way they lived and treated one another. They could then we lights in the world. Paul points to the hope of resurrection and the need to press toward that goal. In the meantime, they could trust the Lord and think about things that were right and noble.

Colossians
Much like Ephesians, Colossians points to the blessings of being in Christ. Christ is preeminent above all, the head of the church, and in Him Christians are made complete. Because of this, Christians are to think on things above, not on on earthly things. Because they are alive in Christ, believers are to live in a way that reflects their full trust in Christ as the Lord.

1 Thessalonians
One of Paul's first epistles, Paul commends these brethren for spreading the gospel. He defends his own work among them, encourages them to live holy lives, and assures them that Christ is coming again. Those who died in Christ were awaiting the resurrection. They all needed to be prepared for the return of Christ and the final judgment.

2 Thessalonians
Some were concerned that the Lord had already come or that He would be coming back immediately. Certain things needed to happen before then, but they were assured that God would vindicate his people who were being persecuted. In the meantime, they needed to stand firm in the teachings they had been given.

1 Timothy
Timothy was a younger coworker of Paul. Paul had left him in Ephesus in order to help the church there. Timothy is encouraged in his work as an evangelist. Paul stresses the need for sound teaching and reliance upon Scripture because there would be some who would stray from the faith.

2 Timothy
Paul was coming to the end of his own life and writes Timothy one last time to encourage him in his work. Timothy was to guard what

was entrusted to him and to follow the pattern of sound teaching he had learned. Christians were not to be quarrelsome, but they were to stand for what is right. Scripture is able to provide the needed spiritual tools to make God's worker complete. Paul would soon be sacrificing his life for Christ.

Titus

Another of Paul's traveling companions, Titus was left in Crete to help set things in order among the disciples. Titus, like Timothy, was to help appoint elders in the church there so that they could be led properly. Titus, too, was to stress the sound teaching of Scripture, to be ready for every good work, and to avoid the pitfalls of error.

Philemon

A man named Onesimus had been a slave of Philemon and had run away. Philemon had become a Christian, and when Onesimus left, he, too became a Christian. Paul had become close to both o them, so Paul pleaded with Philemon to take Onesimus back as a brother in Christ. This shows how relationships can change when people turn to Christ.

General Letters

Hebrews

Hebrews is an anonymous letter written to encourage Jewish Christians at the time to remain faithful to Jesus. Because of persecution, many were tempted to return to their former ways in Judaism. The writer shows how everything in Christ is better since Christ was the fulfillment of the old covenant. He shows how the old contained many shadows and types that were completed in Christ. For instance, the animal sacrifices in the old covenant were fulfilled by the ultimate sacrifice of Christ, through whom is true forgiveness and access into presence of God.

James
James, the brother of Jesus, writes this letter to Christians as a practical encouragement to listen to Scripture, treat others properly by not showing partiality, and show their faith by how they act toward others. The letter contrasts the wisdom of the world with the wisdom of God. James encourages his readers to be careful with how they speak, learn to be humble before God, and be patient and prayerful through trials.

1 Peter
Peter writes to encourage Christians who are undergoing persecution. They are born again to a living hope and can rejoice in their inheritance reserved in heaven. Even though they suffer trials, they can trust God for salvation. Because of the trials, they needed to be determined to keep a good example before others and be ready to suffer more if needed.

2 Peter
Peter here warns about false teachers who would come in among the people and cause many problems. Christians needed to grow in God's grace and knowledge, determined to become stronger so that they don't stumble. There would be those who scoff at the idea that God would bring judgment on the world. God is patient, however, and wants all to repent. Yet there would come the time that God judges and ushers in the new heavens and new earth.

1 John
John encourages fellowship in Christ by walking in the light of God's will. Christians are to avoid sin, but they can have confidence that Jesus is their advocate. John stresses love for God and one another, and also accepting the truth about Jesus Christ coming in the flesh. They were to test all teachers by what they said about Jesus and seek to abide in the truth of Jesus. By loving God and obeying His commandments by faith, God assures Christians can overcome the world.

2 John

John here briefly warns about false teachers regarding Jesus Christ. Christians are to love one another and seek to abide in the teaching of Christ. Those who do not do so are not to be given fellowship.

3 John

John writes to encourage Gaius in his work with the church where he lived. Sadly, a man named Diotrephes wanted to dominate over the Christians there and he refused to acknowledge the authority of the apostles. John indicates he will deal with the problem. In the meantime, they were to imitate what is good.

Jude

Jude wanted to write a letter about the common salvation of Christians, but was compelled to write to contend for the faith because there were false teachers who were secretly bringing in destructive doctrines among Christians. They needed to be identified and avoided, for they would be judged. Christians needed to stay true to the faith and do whatever was needed to save others.

Revelation

The apostle John writes to seven churches of Asia minor (where modern Turkey is). Christ had a message for each church, identifying both positive and negative people, doctrines, and attitudes found in each. For some, they needed to repent; for others, they needed to remain faithful. The book is filled with symbolic language that is geared toward showing that there is a great war between Christ with His armies and the devil with his forces. There are signs showing that powerful government forces (like Rome) would persecute the people of God. However, the point of the book is that Christ will always be triumphant and His people will be vindicated. A final judgment will render reward and punishment accordingly. The language in Revelation relies heavily on Old Testament books like Ezekiel, Daniel, and Zechariah.